The Theatre of Garc
Text, Performance, Psych

The Theatre of García Lorca offers radical new readings of his major plays, drawing on cultural studies, women's and gay studies, psychoanalysis, and previously unexamined archival material. It provides fascinating historical accounts of productions in different times and places, from New York in the 1930s to Madrid in the 1980s. It also juxtaposes Lorca with major figures such as Gregorio Marañón, Langston Hughes, André Gide, and Lluís Pasqual, enabling us to see his theater in a new light. In addition, the book presents a new psychoanalytic reading of the plays that returns to Freud's early clinical texts.

Examining the complex and productive intersection of history and fantasy that is characteristic both of García Lorca's theater and of the cult to which it has given rise, this study offers a thorough reassessment of Lorca's work.

Paul Julian Smith is the Professor of Spanish at the University of Cambridge and head of the Department of Spanish and Portuguese. He has published eight books on Spanish and Latin American literature and cinema.

The Theatre of García Lorca

Text, Performance, Psychoanalysis

PAUL JULIAN SMITH

CAMBRIDGE
UNIVERSITY PRESS

CAMBRIDGE UNIVERSITY PRESS
Cambridge, New York, Melbourne, Madrid, Cape Town, Singapore, São Paulo

Cambridge University Press
The Edinburgh Building, Cambridge CB2 8RU, UK

Published in the United States of America by Cambridge University Press, New York

www.cambridge.org
Information on this title: www.cambridge.org/9780521622929

First published 1998
This digitally printed version 2008

A catalogue record for this publication is available from the British Library

Library of Congress Cataloguing in Publication data
Smith, Paul Julian.
The theatre of García Lorca : text, performance, psychoanalysis /
Paul Julian Smith.
p.   cm. – (Cambridge studies in Latin American and Iberian
literature ; 14)
Includes bibliographical references and index.
ISBN 0-521-62292-1 (hardbound)
1. García Lorca, Federico, 1898–1936 – Criticism and
interpretation.   2. García Lorca, Federico, 1898–1936 – Stage
history.   I. Title.   II. Series.
PQ6613.A763Z88532   1998
862′ .62 – dc21   97-38634
                                                          CIP

ISBN 978-0-521-62292-9 hardback
ISBN 978-0-521-05746-2 paperback

quince años

Contents

Preface

I thank the following libraries and archives: in Madrid the Fundación García Lorca (especially the librarians Sonia González García and Rosa María Juan de Haro), the Real Academia de la Medicina, the Fundación Juan March, the Biblioteca Nacional, and the Filmoteca Nacional; in New York the Public Library at Lincoln Center; in Paris the Bibliothèque de l'Arsenal (especially Mme. Paule Tourniac); in London the Wellcome Institute, the British Film Institute, the British Library, and the University Library at Senate House; in Cambridge the University Library.

Emilie Bergmann, Tracy Jermyn, and Chris Perriam kindly provided me with materials on García Lorca. Ros Ribas kindly sent a portfolio of excellent production photos. My greatest debt is to María Delgado, who asked me to write what became the first half of Chapter 4 for *Contemporary Theatre Review* and kindly provided me with a large number of press clippings and videotapes without which that chapter could not have been written.

Chapter 2 was read and published in 1996 in a slightly different form as the fourth Paper in Spanish Theatre History, produced by the Spanish Theatre Research Project in the Department of Hispanic Studies in Queen Mary and Westfield College, University of London. Chapter 4 was read as a lecture at the State University of New York at Stony Brook, the Instituto Cervantes (Manchester, England), and New York University. Finally, I thank students and faculty who have attended short courses I have taught on García Lorca's theater at Johns Hopkins University, Baltimore, Maryland; Washington University, St Louis, Missouri; and the University of Cambridge. In order to ensure a readable text in one language, I have translated all quotation from Castilian, Catalan, and French and give references in the original only for García Lorca's own work.

Illustrations

Photo credits and permissions

1 Billy Rose Theatre Collection: New York Public Library for the Performing Arts; Astor, Lenox, and Tilden foundations

2 Agence de Presse Bernand, Paris

TVE did not reply to my request to reproduce Figure 4, which was provided by the Fundación Federico García Lorca.

Introduction
Text, Performance, Psychoanalysis

In 1994 the Fundación Federico García Lorca moved to new quarters in Madrid, next door to the Residencia de Estudiantes, of which García Lorca himself had been the most celebrated student. There, under the direction of García Lorca's nephew Manuel Fernández-Montesinos, the Fundación continued its academic activities – publishing a specialist journal that featured a wide range of contributors and approaches, editing catalogues of its invaluable manuscript holdings, organizing international symposia on the poet.[1]

In 1995 the Huerta de San Vicente outside Granada was opened as a "Museum-House" (*Casa-Museo*) dedicated to García Lorca. Purchased eleven years before by the town council, it was filled with "furniture, pictures, and original objects from the house as it was when García Lorca lived in it," at a time when he composed some of his best-known plays and poems.[2] At the opening ceremony García Lorca's niece Isabel García Lorca played the poet's arrangement of a popular song on his own piano. *El País* reported that the Museum "seal[ed] the reconciliation between García Lorca and Granada," and that together with the birthplace in Fuentevaqueros (also a museum to the poet)[3] and the Fuente de Lágrimas ("Spring of Tears") of Alfacar, where the poet's remains are believed to lie, the Huerta de San Vicente "complete[d] a Lorcan route" or tourist trail.[4]

The Fundación, with its catalogues and manuscripts, the Huerta and birthplace with their relics and collectibles ("Letters from Granada: Number 1 in an Epistolary Series"), each seems to signify in its different way the definitive institutionalization of García Lorca in Spain, the poet's consolidation as an academic and a popular icon on the verge of the centenary of his birth. Moreover, *El País*'s stress on "reconciliation" suggests the final termination of an

extended period of mourning, one marked by the full incorporation of García Lorca into the Madrid academy and the Granadan
establishment toward which in his lifetime he felt such ambivalence: Isabel García Lorca is reported to have wept on hearing the
address by Laura García Lorca de los Ríos, the director of the
Huerta, in which she presented the house as "an extension of the
body [of the poet], an extension of his imagination."

Outside Spain also it appeared that García Lorca had achieved
an untouchable status – for example, it was reported that in the
United Kingdom he had surpassed Brecht as the most performed
foreign playwright.[5] Yet it is a commonplace of cultural studies that
any public figure (writer, politician, movie star) is a site of struggle.
And one aim of this book is to examine the constitution of what I
have called elsewhere the "author function" in relation to García
Lorca,[6] to tease out those contradictions that trouble the smooth
surface of institutional prestige and historical reconciliation. More
specifically, the increasing acknowledgment of García Lorca's
homosexuality must problematize the very notion of a "legacy" of
García Lorca that is to be preserved and consecrated by family,
region, and nation-state. Lesbian or gay artists whose relationships
remain invisible or unrecognized by law may not be best served by
those who legally inherit what remains of their name and property.
As Luis Fernández Cifuentes has persuasively argued, it was the
nature of García Lorca to seduce.[7] And this seduction (etymologically, "leading astray") means that García Lorca's life and work are
irreducible to bare facts, "original objects," or plot synopses. But
this need not mean that the glamour of his figure or the rapture
produced by and celebrated in his work can simply be assigned to
an ineffable "magic" or *duende*. Rather, I will suggest that this shut-
tling between concept and affect (between thought and feeling) so
characteristic of García Lorca's theater should itself be submitted
to analysis, and most specifically to psychoanalysis as the vocabulary of passion, in all senses of the word. As we shall see, passion,
like seduction, leads to the greatest of threats and of pleasures –
the loss of a sense of self (of García Lorca's and of our own).

Cultural studies as a discipline is only now emerging in Peninsu-

lar Hispanism.[8] But if, as has been recently argued, "the modernizing project" of Spain in the 1920s and 1930s involving the "incorporation of popular and mass cultural forms particularly marked
. . . the Spanish avant garde,"[9] and if García Lorca's work is itself
characterized by both "avant garde experimentalism and traditional elements,"[10] then García Lorca must remain a key figure in
any new approach to Spanish culture, as he was in more traditional
literary studies. In my stress, then, on the historical, commercial,
and ideological conditions of García Lorca's "production" (of his
self and of his theater), I thus seek to make a contribution to this
emerging field. However, unlike many practitioners of performance studies and some theater professionals who engage in
"director's theater," I do not contest the importance of the text.[11]
And if the 1990s have seen an institutionalization of García Lorca
in Spain at least, they have also seen a number of publications that
have changed the corpus of García Lorca's writing and will perhaps
transform our present understanding of its canonicity. Thus we
have seen the appearance, much delayed, of three substantial col-
lections of juvenilia – prose, poetry, and drama;[12] of the first free-
standing edition of the *Sonetos del amor oscuro* (*Sonnets of Dark Love*),
previously included only in the last edition of the complete works;[13]
and the first Spanish edition of the unproduced film script *Viaje a
la luna* (*Journey to the Moon*) based on access to the original manuscript.[14] There is little doubt that further unpublished works held
by the Fundación will emerge.

The misadventures of García Lorca's manuscript have by now a
long history: If *Viaje a la luna* had appeared in both complete and
incomplete form in English translation before it did so in the Spanish original, then, notoriously, *El público* (*The Public*) had been the
object of a full-length critical monograph in both Spanish and
English before permission was finally given for the text itself to appear.[15] The precedence of commentary over original in this case is
a deconstructive irony noted by critics such as Fernández Cifuentes.[16] But this postponed publication is the clearest case of a di-
vergence between the playwright and the family that inherited his
copyright – for García Lorca had published in his lifetime the most

explicitly homoerotic fragment of the play, the dialogue of the Figure of Bells and the Figure of Vine Leaves; and he had repeatedly
insisted that *El público* and the other "unplayable" plays constituted
his real, true theater.

There has thus been increasing critical interest in García Lorca's
experimental plays, a change of emphasis that is reflected in this
book by the fact that I devote half of my study to them.[17] And there
seems little doubt that an earlier publication of the unplayable plays
would have counteracted the pernicious and pervasive folkloric
stereotypes that still determine foreign responses to García Lorca:
The recently revised *Oxford Companion to the Theatre* simply fails to
mention the experimental plays, focusing, as ever, on the so-called
rural trilogy.[18] If the "impossible" theater was, as García Lorca
declared, destined for the future, we are now that audience, and we
have an ethical responsibility to respond to its challenge, a responsibility which earlier generations of scholars and theatergoers were
denied. Such a burden cannot leave us indifferent, intellectually or
aesthetically.

In tandem with this revision of the corpus of García Lorca's theater comes the proliferation of critical approaches. While the history of what has been called "the politics of theory in post-Franco
Spain"[19] has meant that Spanish criticism remains predominantly
within its linguistic and philological tradition, U.S. scholars in particular have produced a wide range of readings, in addition to the
exemplary historical and textual work of, say, Christopher Maurer
and Andrew A. Anderson – a contemporary scholar or student can
pick and choose among feminist, gay, and deconstructive García
Lorcas, to cite only the most familiar.[20] In this study I generally con-
fine to the footnotes my references to the massive body of preex-
isting criticism in order to leave a clear space for my own argument
and for close reading of the texts themselves.

It is in these close readings that I formulate some controversial
interpretations of four major plays, which I take in reverse order of
composition and increasing order of conceptual complexity and
antinaturalism. Thus of *Yerma* I argue that the central, sterile protagonist can be read as an "intersexual type," and that when she

strangles her husband at the climax of the play she is, following Gregorio Marañón's recommendation to Spaniards of García Lorca's time, suffocating the seeds of the opposite sex that lie deep within her. *Bodas de sangre* (*Blood Wedding*), I argue, dramatizes a lost object or relation – the young male body and its confrontation with that of the other, a mutual penetration of "two men in love," as Langston Hughes's translation puts it. This confrontation cannot be staged by García Lorca but is, much later, by Carlos Saura in his flamenco film version, which I examine in Chapter 4. In *Así que pasen cinco años* (*When Five Years Have Passed*) the hesitations of the protagonist, his postponed engagement and deferred desires, are read as characteristic of the Gidian youth, more desired than desiring, unable or unwilling to integrate romantic love and genital pleasure. Finally, in *El público,* I argue, in the context of Lluís Pasqual's production, for a connection between the play's twin arguments on theater and on homosexuality, a connection that focuses on the perilous and provisional status of both, caught as they are between the subjective and the social, the personal and the public.

My readings are thus dependent on four successive intertexts – writers who are diverse not only in themselves but also in the nature of the relation between them and García Lorca. Thus Gregorio Marañón, Spain's most famous doctor, was a friend of García Lorca's and attended private readings and public performances of his plays. I cite him, however, as the theorist of intersexual states, a theory linked to but distinct from Freud's hypothesis of universal bisexuality and that has complex and productive implications for fertility, feminism, and male homosexuality. Langston Hughes, luminary of the Harlem Renaissance, was the translator of *Bodas de sangre* and of García Lorca's poetry; and the director of a recent New York production of that play cites their similar "interests and passions."[21] I myself am more concerned to show the differences between Hughes's translation and the unpublished version by José Weissberger performed in 1935, differences that reassert discreetly but emphatically a poetic tension and a homoeroticism absent or excluded from the text as it was performed. I also contrast Hughes's practice as a tragic playwright with that of García Lorca. There is some evidence that García Lorca was familiar with Gide's early apology for homosexuality; certainly the title *Corydon* is cited by Rafael Rodríguez Rapún in his one surviving letter to García Lorca. I do not aim to prove that García Lorca drew on this work (published in Spanish with a hostile introduction by Marañón) but rather appeal to it in order to establish a framework within which to reconcile García Lorca's appeal to a natural paradigm with the highly artificial reversals and inversions of *Así que pasen cinco años*. Finally, Lluís Pasqual is the best-known modern director of García Lorca in the Spanish state and the European Union. My last chapter seeks to show how text and staging are inseparable in his productions. But it also suggests that Pasqual's complex relationship with García Lorca is the model for a new kind of identification with the playwright – one that addresses both regionalism and homosexuality with intelligence and humor.

The homosocial confrontation I stage between García Lorca and these four figures (Marañón, Hughes, Gide, and Pasqual) thus leads me beyond literature into other disciplinary discourses, most particularly politics and medicine. My aim here is at once sociopolitical and literary-aesthetic: It is both to open the theatrical text out onto those historical contexts within which it finds its meaning and to lead back nonliterary discourses, such as science, to the literary forms they repudiate but whose traces persist in them nonetheless. Thus while Gide brings literary technique to scientific material in his artful dialogue on biology and evolution, Marañón renders science poetic in his persistent appeal to natural metaphors shared with García Lorca – the tilling of fields, the flooding of streams, the voice that speaks in the blood.

If Spanish cultural studies is still in its infancy, then the same is true of performance studies. Both scholars and theater professionals have lamented the lack of resources in Spain itself – there is no video collection of modern productions; no company dedicated to exploring and renewing the corpus of García Lorca's or Valle Inclán's work; and the annual number of productions of twentieth-century Spanish plays declined dramatically in the 1980s.[22] Spaniards frequently contrast this state of affairs with the more congenial atmosphere they believe to exist in other European countries.

In contrast to a certain strand of performance studies that is biased toward informal productions, often improvisational in form or mounted in nontraditional locations, I restrict myself in this book to theatrical performances of a conventional kind. I thus take four geographical places and historical moments as exemplary or symptomatic of the varied production history of García Lorca.

The first is the best known and thus the least discussed by me: Spain in the 1930s. While Spanish theater of the 1920s has been described as "mediocre and old-fashioned" by European standards,[23] the combination of avant-garde experimentalism and the renovation of traditional forms had by the time of the Republic produced a vital and varied dramatic scene. I focus particularly on the polemic over the 1934 premiere of *Yerma,* a polemic that recurred in a different form in the last days of the Dictatorship with Víctor García and Nuria Espert's iconoclastic production of the same play. My second place and moment is Broadway in the same decade. Here the Neighborhood Playhouse production of *Bodas de sangre* (the first staging of a García Lorca play in the United States) is read within the context of a Broadway still recovering from the Depression and whose critics are often hostile to what they perceive as the pretensions of "little theater" – artistic, mannered, and overly reliant on music and mime. Significant here is the appearance of fully fledged stereotypes of García Lorca and of his theater (of precious lyricism on the one hand and of telluric elementalism on the other) that persist into our own time. A recent multicultural New York production is also examined for the purposes of comparison. The third moment is France in the 1950s and 1960s, when popular biographies and a large number of theatrical productions gave rise to a García Lorca cult or myth based, as elsewhere, on a curious mix of folkloric Hispanophilia and universalist abstraction.[24] The troubled 1958 premiere of *Así que pasen cinco años* (adapted by García Lorca's friend and biographer Marcelle Auclair) is also read (like the New York *Bodas de sangre*) in the context of the struggle between the conflicting priorities of commercial playhouses and a Left Bank or "quality" theater whose artistic tendencies provoked violent reactions in critics.

Finally I address the figure of García Lorca in 1980s Spain, tracing his cinematic profile in biopics and adaptations, before giving an account of Pasqual's publicly funded productions in the various institutional contexts of Barcelona, Madrid, and Paris. García Lorca's legacy is here subject to multiple and contradictory readings, only some of which are reducible to Socialist cultural policy in the period. As in the 1930s, however, García Lorca's productions become the nexus of varied artistic projects, more or less directly connected to the plays themselves – thus Pasqual's *El público*, produced initially for the Centro Dramático Nacional, of which he was director, gave rise not only to Fabià Puigserver's radical staging but also to Ros Ribas's impressionistic production photographs (far superior to conventional press shots) and Frederic Amat's obsessively repeated paintings of top hats and horses, only a tiny proportion of which were used in the posters and program.[25] If it is indeed the case that, as John Hooper suggests, "without government subsidy it is very likely that drama in Spain would have entered a fatal downward spiral in the 1980s,"[26] it is Pasqual's achievement to have created almost *ex nihilo* a performance tradition of the unplayable plays, helped perhaps by Miguel Narros's earlier productions of *Así que pasen cinco años* in 1978 and 1989, which I discuss in Chapter 3. It is an achievement comparable to that of another Madrid-based initiative of the Socialist government, the Centro Nacional de Teatro Clásico (National Center of Classical Theater), established in 1986, which has also sought to re-create a modern tradition whose roots in the past have been violently severed from the present.[27]

There is thus a sense of fragility in performance studies, a pathos and an uncertainty due to the lack of an artifact that survives the event itself, such as one finds in the case of a cinema screening. I have attempted to supply this lack through reference to still photography or video where available. But my main resource is press notices. These may frequently be impressionistic, anecdotal, or inaccurate (such as the New York critics who referred in 1935 to "Lorco"); but they provide invaluable and as yet insufficiently exploited evidence for the aesthetic preferences and ideological prejudices of their age. I thus use press material extensively, but critically, to point up the production and consumption of the figure of García Lorca and the image of his theater in the United States, France, and Spain itself. As I have suggested earlier, this figure and this image remain disturbingly consistent, if internally contradictory, from one period and one place to another, thus suggesting that they are the product of deep-rooted fantasies about nationality and sexuality, fantasies that it may prove impossible to dispel. For theater is both singular and collective, the audience at once isolated and juxtaposed in the darkened auditorium. We are thus both free to fantasize during the performance and inevitably exposed to the public commentaries purveyed by the mass media that precede and underwrite that private experience. In just such a way, psychoanalysis shifts between the subjective and the intersubjective – the psychic formation of the individual and his or her socialization in the collectivity. Public performance, whether it is understood as "theatrical" in the restricted sense or as the acting out of prescribed social roles, is thus connected in complex but undeniable ways to what psychoanalysis's first patient baptized the "private theater" of the psyche.[28]

Why, then, the return to Freud in this book? I have already suggested that, in its twin stress on the psychic and the social, psychoanalysis is particularly appropriate to the study of drama. Beyond this methodological conformity, however, there is a theoretical choice: Given, on the one hand, the apparent exhaustion of Lacanian or *Screen* theory, threatened as it is by a newly vigorous cultural studies and historicism, and, on the other, the popularity of semi-academic Freud bashing that has led even historians of psychoanalysis to concede that "Freud [is] on trial,"[29] it is vital to return once more to Freud's own words. It is for this reason that I have generally chosen not to cite commentary on Freud, be it Marxist, Lacanian, or feminist. If it is indeed the case, as Alan Sinfield argues, that the Freudian corpus is so large and complex as selectively to support almost any interpretation,[30] my own reading coincides with that of Jeremy Tambling, who argues in his important book on confession that "far from colluding with forms of confessional knowledge, [psychoanalysis] has the capacity to put into question precisely the repressions and interdictions forming the basis of religious confession and societal restraint."[31] This is vital for a figure such as García Lorca, whose works, even at their most hermetic, have often been interpreted violently as a personal testimony that betrays the secrets of their creator's soul, a soul that is then made to serve as a prison for the libidinal body of the drama. Hence if I draw in this book not on Freud's literary or cultural texts but on his clinical or metapsychological works, it is not because I seek, as some previous critics have, to pathologize García Lorca or his characters; indeed, a psychoanalytic reading, as I understand it, must transcend both author and protagonist. It is, rather, because my model of theater is comparable to one of Freud's models of the psyche – an economy of drives and desires in which differing quantities of energy are made manifest in subtly varied qualities of affect. Psychoanalysis can thus attempt to incorporate at a theoretical level the most delicate, fragile, and pleasurable aspect of the theatrical experience – dramatic rhythm.

Contrary to the authoritarianism of which he has stereotypically been accused, Freud consistently refuses to draw a simple dividing line between neurotics and perverts on the one hand and "normal" subjects on the other. Taking his lead, I draw on linked pairs of terms in each chapter in order to give a general account of psychic and dramatic processes in each play that is related but not reducible to that play's narrative content. In *Yerma* I focus on anxiety and bisexuality. "Anxiety" is a liminal term, variously positioned, as Freud develops his theory of mind, between the present and the past, the real and the fantastic, the somatic and the psychic, the constitutional and the accidental. Bisexuality, for Freud, constitutes the "highest degree of complexity" in such fantasies, provoking such theatrical phenomena as the "play[ing of] both parts" in the sexual relation, a "simultaneity of contradictory actions" or "constant switching . . . as though on to an adjoining track" that is also a key to the dramatic complexity of García Lorca's theater.[32] In *Bodas de sangre* I focus on mourning, melancholia,[33] and masochism. While these psychic phenomena correspond to the action of the play (with its grieving women ever anxious, as Freud puts it, "to turn [their] cheek whenever there is a chance of receiving a blow"[34]), what interests me more is the process of introjection or incorporation that they share – in melancholia (for Freud a pathological form of mourning), the ego takes into itself the lost object it has loved too dearly; in moral masochism, the internalized parental prohibition forms the basis of a dark Destiny, externalized once more but "linked to [internal] libidinal ties" ("Masochism," p. 423). In such circumstances pleasure and unpleasure become an "economic problem" – "the temporal sequence of changes, rises and falls in the quantity of stimulus" ("Masochism," p. 414). It is a rhythmic pattern mimicked by *Bodas de sangre*'s fluctuating dramatic action.

In the case of *Así que pasen cinco años*, read so often as a "case study" of its author's supposed neuroses, I reread Freud's versions of anamnesis (the patient's version of his or her own sickness) and of identification (the process by which the subject is transformed by his or her assumption of an image of an other). Like Freud's archaeologist, suspending judgment and working in inverse chronological order through the psychic strata,[35] García Lorca also sets up a recursive or inverted dynamic in which we must "remember towards tomorrow"; or again like Freud's reluctant patient Dora, who (Freud finally claims) identifies with her beloved father in his love for his married mistress, so (I argue) García Lorca's protagonist, who cannot experience desire for a woman, identifies with his Fiancée in her passion for a mute masculine figure. It is not simply, then, that the round dance of partnering in Dora's case anticipates García Lorca's multiple and nonreciprocal couples; or that both Freud's and García Lorca's narratives are based, like Gide's *Corydon*, on the postponement of marriages; it is rather that identification, in the full sense, must lead to a problematization of subjectivity: of the sense of self expressed so haltingly, fragmentarily, and painfully in the anamnesis.

The final chapter is the most historical, devoted as most of it is to the cultural analysis of the figure of García Lorca in Socialist Spain. In my reading of Pasqual's *El público*, however, I attempt to integrate psychoanalysis with staging – thus the movement of the actors' bodies in and out of the lighting design suggests once more that process of projection and introjection typical of melancholia; and Freud's complex reading of the relation between homosexuality and group identification is mirrored in the costumes and performance styles of the play's multiple and elusive protagonists, alternately merging into a group and separating into individuals, now aggressive and jealous, now tender and loving. As *El público* shows, when male rivals become love objects then a new space opens up for a "remarkable thing" – a homosexual object choice without a feminine attitude.[36]

Some may still feel it is inappropriate to speak of García Lorca in such terms, citing the poet's supposed anti-intellectualism. Yet my reading is not only prefigured by a certain psychoanalytical turn among other García Lorca critics; it is also sanctioned by Rafael Martínez Nadal's study of *El público* some twenty years ago, which attacks the stereotype of a García Lorca who sings "like a bird on a tree" and vindicates the playwright's density of "cultural allusions" and "preoccupation with ethical and aesthetic ideas."[37] Certainly my own aim in discussing the theme of homosexuality, which remains as frequently disavowed in Spain as it is acknowledged,[38] is both to attack such stereotypes as García Lorca's supposed "sense of frustration" and "uncanny understanding of the female mind"[39] and to insert García Lorca's work into a broader conceptual arena from which both Hispanism and cultural history in general will benefit. To take one example, there has been almost no "queering" of García Lorca in Spain, no contemporary appropriation of his historical figure comparable to, say, in a black British context Isaac Julien's erotic film meditation on Langston Hughes.[40] Or again, on a more academic level, Alan Sinfield in Britain once more has recently devoted a book to *The Wilde Century,* in which he investigates the implications for contemporary gay men of Oscar's life, work, and death. A García Lorca centennial is also just cause for a "García Lorca century," an investigation of what meaning another, later sacrifice bears for a problematic present.

Sinfield's position is exemplary in that he refuses both to read back contemporary homosexuality into the invisibility and silences of previous decades and to project forward earlier versions of "same-sex passion" (his preferred, non-anachronistic term) into a present where they no longer have any purchase. And, coincidentally, in this perverse process of cultural history (whereby Wilde can be recognized retrospectively as a homosexual only because of the effeminate paradigm that he himself introduced) it is on a persistent Lorcan concern, the question of queer manliness, that Sinfield also concentrates. Thus just as the two Figures of *El público* are torn between competing versions of masculinity, so Wilde initiates a paradigm shift between nineteenth-century versions of same-sex passion as quintessentially masculine (*The Wilde Century*, p. vii) and the twentieth-century identification of homosexuality with effeminacy. This new mapping of a "contorted variation" of the masculine/feminine binary onto lesbians and gay men is developed (for Sinfield) by Freud, whose "cross-sex grid" seeks to fix homosexuality as identification with the opposite sex even as it separates sexual practices from gender (pp. 161–2).

It is thus that there is a split in British fiction of the early part of the century between athletes and aesthetes (between masculine-identified objects and feminine-identified subjects), a split that recurs quite clearly in the contrast between the rugged physique of the Rugby Player and the delicate sensitivity of the Young Man in García Lorca's *Así que pasen cinco años*. Hence if García Lorca, like his contemporaries Gide or E. M. Forster, at times repudiates the effeminate stereotype and at others seems to take it on, it is because that stereotype was only then superimposing itself on an earlier queer manliness, and the two incompatible identifications were making themselves felt alternately and simultaneously, like a doubly exposed photograph. This is also the explanation for the apparent transparency of García Lorca's effeminacy and the genuine surprise felt by his friends at the revelation of his homosexuality after his death – for still in the Spain of the 1920s or 1930s a man who intermittently flaunted a parody of women's dress or who was caricatured as a "mama's boy" was not necessarily branded with

that homosexual object choice which was for Freud the conse-
quence of a feminine identification.[41] It is for this reason that I
agree with Christopher Maurer when he writes in his introduction
to the prose juvenilia that the themes of the "carnal Calvary" and
of "impossible love" cannot simply be read as homosexuality in the
modern sense. More than mere social prohibition (however violently imposed), they suggest a desire that, even after Wilde, can be
only imperfectly defined, imperfectly named.[42]

The visitors' leaflet to the Museum-House of the Huerta de San
Vicente reprints only one poem – the "Gacela del amor que no se
deja ver" ("Poem of Love Which Does Not Allow Itself to Be
Seen"), which includes the lines "me abrasaba en tu cuerpo/sin
saber de quién era" ("I burned up in your body/without knowing
whose body it was"). It is an elegant, and in this context unexpected, plea for the pleasures of invisibility, anonymity, and prom-
iscuity. If theater is, like the Museum itself, an "extension of the
body of the poet," then this is a fine image of the audience,
wrapped in silence and cloaked in darkness, all the better to con-
ceal and to enjoy its guilty pleasures. A further example of the passion of the audience suggests itself – an elegiac juvenile prose text
called "Mi primer amor" ("My First Love"), in which the author
pines over a faded photograph of a long-dead girl, only to neglect
her when subjected to the more urgent demands of unspecified
carnality.[43] For Hispanists, Hispanophiles, and theatergoers also
the image of García Lorca, as reflected in such faded photographs
as those reprinted by the Granada Museums on their postcards,
has served as a first love. One challenge posed by García Lorca's
theater, then, is the integration of the romantic fantasy of the lost
object (which is clearly too powerful to be eradicated) with the
more immediate drives and passions of drama as it is experienced
in performance. The unfillable gap that opens up between the
demand of love and the gratification of need is what Lacan called
"desire."[44] This constitutive imbalance is not only a further psychoanalytic model of the dramatic process. It is also a fitting image
of the historical hesitancies of the García Lorca who has recently
been named as "the paradigmatic Spanish modernist":

. . . because of the ambivalence of his response to modernity, because of his inability to translate his political sympathies into direct political action, and because neither of these things prevented him from becoming a Republican martyr.[45]

It is between modernity and tradition, between passion and action, that Yerma and the doctors also play out their drama of differing desires.

1

Yerma and the Doctors
García Lorca, Marañón,
and the Anxiety of Bisexuality

1. The Voice of Blood

Yerma, García Lorca's tragic poem of the sterile woman, has provoked problems of interpretation. Thus while one critic views the
main character as a tragic heroine whose final strangling of her
husband is "triumphant and liberating,"[1] another sees her as "a
murderess condemned to an eternity of barrenness."[2] Or again
some critics claim that Yerma "aspires to cross the gender barrier
and elude . . . the constrictions that a paternalistic and reactionary
society imposes on [her]";[3] another advises that she should "yield
to [her husband] Juan [and] become 'tronchada y rota' [bent and
broken]" for him, thus "open[ing] herself to the Dionysiac."[4] This
last critic draws a normalizing "lesson from psychoanalysis" –
"repression of the libido is dangerous to the psyche" (p. 130); but
one editor of the play claims that Yerma's "problem is simply, ter-
ribly biological."[5]

The rural setting of *Yerma* and García Lorca's frequent appeal to
lyrical and often liquid imagery drawn from the natural or organic
worlds (to streams and clouds, to blood and milk) have tended to
reconfirm such elemental readings of the play, whether they are
based on a psychic model of libido as hydraulic pressure that must
seek release or a hypostatization of nature as cosmic principle that
cannot be eluded. What I shall argue in this opening chapter, however, is that neither the psyche nor biology is as "simple" as critics
have claimed. Indeed, critical controversy, which is founded ulti-
mately on differing perceptions of the relation between the personal and the social, is echoed by the contradictory views of natural

16

and human law expressed by characters within the play, views that (by the end) remain unresolved, defiantly open.

García Lorca once said in connection with *Yerma* that "blood has no voice."[6] However, his play is concerned precisely with the intersection of the somatic and the linguistic, with a speaking of and in the woman's body. One way out of the interminable content-based controversies (on, for example, whether husband or wife should take the blame for Yerma's failure to conceive) is to read the play's language not as referential but rather as performative. This approach (which pays proper attention to García Lorca's frequently heightened, abstracted diction) suggests that words precede and, perhaps, displace actions – just as the neighbor María is impregnated by the whisper of her husband in her ear, so Yerma's sterility is procured by Juan's silence and denial, his refusal of the fecund word.[7] Another approach, and this is the one I take myself, is that of historicization. It has recently been argued that the fundamental conflict in current criticism (between Yerma as rebellious, willful heroine and Yerma as victim of traditional moral indoctrination) is not simply a modern concern but one topical in the 1930s, when questions of free will, social justice, and ideological determinism were also much debated.[8] But, to my knowledge, no systematic study has been made of the relation of the varied versions of maternity in *Yerma* to those voiced by Spanish doctors in the period. In this chapter I first set the play in the context of gynecology at a time when the increasing medicalization of childbirth and the development of reproductive technology were combined with the idealization of motherhood and the eugenic concern for the "biopower" of the nation. I go on to contrast these conventional doctors (who occupy political positions of both left and right) with the much more distinguished figure of Gregorio Marañón, the most famous Spanish medical specialist of the century. Marañón's vast corpus, complex and contradictory, successively draws on and contributes to the varied disciplines of endocrinology, morphology, and psychology. Just as the medical commonplaces of the period shed unexpected light on *Yerma* (most particularly on the separation or fusion of reproduction and sexual pleasure), so Marañón's more idiosyncratic vision of the hormones, of body types, and of psychic mechanisms suggests a new reading of the play, based on his theory of "intersexual states," states that (Marañón claims) are frequently identical in women with sterility.

Marañón's relation to Freud is complex. While both paid particular attention to physiological and psychic bisexuality, Marañón's biologism had no place for the unconscious or fantasy. Finally, then, I turn to Freud, in whose varied accounts of anxiety and hysteria we find not only (as in Marañón) a symptomatology of Yerma but also a model of the movement from the biological to the social as it is played out both in the subject's anamnesis and in the history of psychoanalysis. My purpose, thus, is not to pathologize Yerma (and even in Marañón the line between the monstrous and natural is blurred); it is rather to trace the halting and shifting boundary between the pathological and the normal traced by the repetitive and lyrical action of the play and the discontinuous development of its main character. In his shifting views on the motives of repression (from real to fantastic), Freud comes finally to abandon "the unfruitful contrast between external and internal factors, between experience and constitution"[9] and with it any simple etiological distinction between the congenital and the experiential. Taking Yerma to the doctors, then, is not to transform the play into a case history; it is rather to place it more fully in a drama of the woman's body contemporary with the play, a drama played out by male clinicians of several disciplines and their female patients.

It is known that Marañón, together with two of his colleagues, attended the controversial premiere of *Yerma* at the Teatro Español in Madrid on 29 December 1934. He was also among a select invited audience to which García Lorca read *La casa de Bernarda Alba* shortly before his death.[10] *Yerma* was bitterly attacked by the right-wing press for its supposed crudity of language and obscenity of subject matter: *ABC* attacked its use of "unnecessary crudity"; *La Epoca* its depiction of "a pathological case of idée fixe, of obsession and madness, to which, unfortunately, nothing is added by [the playwright's] skill, dramatic action, high flown poetic inspiration, or the

scientific description of a morbid case study."[11] But the press was
equally scathing about *Yerma*'s audience: *La Voz* noted the "pale
youths" in García Lorca's retinue; *Gracia y Justicia* the poet's "circle
of [male] friends"; a third journal the "strange brotherhood" that
flocked to the play, shrieking in the intervals and archly gesturing
with "their finger on their cheek."[12] It is a gesture that Marañón,
also, finds typical of the "psychological intersexual" and illustrated
with a photograph of Ludwig of Bavaria.[13] Beyond this blatantly
homophobic and politically motivated prejudice, the medical imaginary of the period provides a connection between the play's subject matter and its audience – for Marañón, most cases of infertility
are "simply" cases of female intersexuality. However, as we shall see,
Marañón's "biological" and evolutionist theories of sexual difference are more complex and contradictory than they at first appear;
and they themselves must be set in the context of the conflict
between archaic and modernizing models of motherhood that had
been waged since the nineteenth century in Spain. It is a conflict
that might be described, in Foucault's words, as that between a symbolics of blood and an analytics of sexuality.

2. Yerma *and the Doctors*

Yerma's village, nameless and timeless, is innocent of modern medicine: Yerma will visit the local wise woman, not a male specialist, in
search of a cure for her infertility. Yet this ruralism represents a significant artistic choice by García Lorca. For the years prior to the
play's composition saw a progressive medicalization of pregnancy
and childbirth in Spain (as elsewhere in Europe), in which enlightened men of science sought to penetrate the darkness even of men
and women from the growing urban proletariat and the rural dis-
possessed. Marañón's famous expedition to las Hurdes, the object
of Buñuel's documentary of 1932, is only the best-known example
of this socially hygienic medical mission.

    Luis S. Granjel's historical sketch of twentieth-century Spanish
medicine stresses the professionalization of the various specialisms
in the early decades – thus 1926 saw the founding of the presti-

gious *Nueva Gaceta Médica* (with Marañón on the editorial board).
Gynecology had been constituted as a discrete branch of surgery in
the second half of the nineteenth century; now pediatrics was
finally separated from it; and 1922 saw the founding of the *Archivos
de la Sociedad Ginecológica Española*.[14] However, María del Carmen
Alvarez Ricart's exhaustively documented study of women in Spanish medicine shows the reverse of this process: The constitution of
the new disciplines of gynecology and obstetrics was effected
through the control of those women who had traditionally taken
care of mothers in childbirth. Midwives were subject to increasing
"professionalization" and required by repeated government edicts
to display evidence of scientific training and to submit to regula-
tion.[15] Medicalization and antifeminism thus went hand in hand.

Other attempts at social hygiene seem more benevolent, initially
at least. Specialists with a social conscience, such as Jesús Sarabia y
Pardo, argued as early as 1893 for "houses of maternity" in which
indigent women would benefit from lower mortality rates; here,
each woman would be isolated from the others in an individual
room or cubicle.[16] Luis Soler y Soto agitated in *El Monitor Sanitario*
of 1911 for institutions in which all pregnant women would be "affectionately" received, thus reducing miscarriages provoked either
by the mothers' "carelessness" or by their hunger.[17] The extension
of the specialists' domain coincided, however, with an increasingly
minute discipline of the woman's body, whatever her class. Thus
Adolfo Martínez Cerecedo in 1904 both claims that the role of the
obstetrician is not confined to the birth itself, extending before and
after that moment, and offers detailed instructions for the future
mother's behavior – she must have sex only in moderation, avoid
"intense emotions," and disinfect daily her genitals and breasts.[18]
Francisco Vidal Solares's "precepts" for pregnant women are tragi-
cally irrelevant to the working class or rural poor – honeymoon trips
are forbidden, lest they cause miscarriage; women are to breathe
"well-oxygenated air" and avoid confined spaces and excessive physical exercise. Even "strong smells" are forbidden.[19] Most important,
however, "the pregnant woman is [both] wholly devoted to the
being lodged inside her" and "must consult her doctor at the slight-

est discomfort" (p. 3). Like the blind, expectant mothers are unable to see their own predicament.

Perhaps the most prolific writer on sterility, both before and after the Civil War, is Vital Aza, author of a lecture published in the proceedings of the Royal Academy of Medicine in 1927 on *The Conduct of the Gynaecologist Towards Female Sterility*.[20] Aza fixes the date of medical intervention as being four years without conception after marriage (p. 421); and he writes that the vast majority of cases of sterility are due to syphilitic infection of one or both parties (p. 422). And as a "woman's confessor," he is in an ideal position to confirm the central proposition García Lorca attributes to Yerma – namely, that "women are more sensitive to the griefs of [frustrated] motherhood, than they are to the [sexual] pleasures of matrimony" (p. 425).

The supposedly pervasive frigidity of women coincided moreover with the rise of new contraceptive and reproductive technologies. Aza fulminates against surgical sterilization and contraceptive devices, a "neo-Malthusian threat" that "haunts" not only society, with their threat to the birth rate, but also the woman's body, in their supposed precipitation of pathological disorders (p. 424). For Aza, the surgical experiments of his predecessors are now anathema: Such operations as the stretching of the cervix were hopelessly ineffective; still, he notes with characteristic optimism, the "surgical phase" of gynecology has given specialists unique visual knowledge of "pathological anatomies" (p. 428). Now it is known (and this is Marañón's great theme) that fertility is hormonally conditioned (p. 429).

But the very advances of scientific knowledge allow perilous possibilities, undreamed of before – artificial insemination may lead to the "moral bankruptcy of the profession" (p. 431) when, as in France, the donor is not the husband. And even the advances in endocrinology, so fundamental to modern Spanish medicine as defined in the period, may have monstrous consequences: Aza cites a paper supposedly given in Stockholm (he gives no bibliographical details) on a monkey that, after receiving a grafted human ovary, had been artificially inseminated with human sperm. The unfortu-

nate animal had died before giving birth, thus sparing the specialists a tricky decision – should the resulting "it" be weaned on milk
or carrot juice? (p. 432). The promise and the menace of the hor-
monal graft recur in a contemporary caricature of another surgeon,
wielding scissors and scalpel. He is accompanied by twin pictures of
his patient – the "before" picture is of an old bearded man slumped
in an armchair, the "after" of a moustachioed muscleman vigor-
ously lifting weights. At the bottom, leering monkeys look on.[21]

Even after the Republic and the Civil War, Aza's tone remains the
same. A popular volume on the causes of female sterility, published
in 1941, makes explicit in a much harsher climate the connection
between technophobia and antifeminism. The increasing recourse
to contraception and abortion is caused by "mistaken ideas about
the rights and duties of women"; or again, artificial insemination,
which may be acceptable in countries with a differing "religious
atmosphere, ethnic inheritance, and geographical latitude," must
be rigorously restricted in Spain.[22] Women who wish to "free themselves from what they consider to be the tiresome servitude of sexual submission to men" are anathema. Inversely, a Spanish husband
will willingly pay for a blood transfusion to save the life of his wife;
he will not contemplate the donation of what Aza coyly calls
"another organic essence" that is equivalent to the "spiritual heart
beat of the soul" (pp. 48, 50). The lyrical vocabulary here ("jugo";
"latido") recurs in García Lorca's hymns to natural motherhood.

There is thus a structural relation between the development of
reproductive technology (which doctors take care to keep out of
the hands of women who are "blind" to its monstrous potentiali-
ties), the promotion of nationalist, eugenicist hygiene (which
equates family and race), and the idealization of motherhood in
the face of the feminist claims to reproductive autonomy precipi-
tated by that self-same male-generated technology. It is no accident
that Aza's lyrical invocation to motherhood is agricultural, in spite
of his own urban practice:

It has now become possible to render abundant and fertile female
ground which was hitherto arid and sterile. Gynecological farmers

[know that] the better tilled the earth which is to receive the seed, the straighter and deeper the furrow, the easier and more abundant will be the harvest. . . . And in the same way that one does not wait until it is time to sow the seed before turning over the soil, one must not delay in tackling the problem of female sterility . . . until a marriage proves to be infertile. . . . Rather, preparing in advance the desired result [*fruto*], the woman's organic land will be worked over from childhood, tilling the girl's tiny plot, and pulling out the weeds which may later steal her vital essence [*jugo*]. . . . In the girl of today, the mother of tomorrow must be saved. (p. 32)

The tone is reminiscent of Victor's advice to the "dry" farmer Juan that he offers Yerma: "Get him to dig deep" ("Que ahonde" [I, 1, 43]). But the many perils or inhibitions to reproductive development are also stressed by Marañón, in the rather different context of his doctrine of organic bi- or intersexuality.

Paradoxically, then, women must be subjected to lifelong discipline and punishment (by both doctors and mothers) if they are properly to realize that reproductive mission that is their unique, natural, and inevitable role. Motherhood, ideal and abstract, must be protected from modernity. Thus Luis Soler's lecture entitled simply "Motherhood," read to the Sociedad Española de Higiene on the eve of the Civil War, both praises maternity as "woman's most sublime act, the basis of the family and of racial hygiene" as predestined by the Supreme Creator and laments the deplorable state of the race, threatened as it is by "the modern trends" of free love, divorce, contraception, and sterilization – social struggle must give way to creation, and female emancipation to the immutable laws of nature.[23] Once more the appeal to rural imagery recurs – woman has become a sexual "trough" in which men satiate their animal instincts (p. 25).

It is perhaps significant that at a moment when doctors were claiming that for the first time in history the barren woman could be made to bear fruit, García Lorca should write a play on the theme of irredeemable sterility. And yet there are hints in the first act of this scientific revolution: Yerma notes to her neighbor María that a third woman has taken three years to conceive; and in the old days, the times of her mother, women took much longer ("Elena tardó tres años, y otras antiguas, del tiempo de mi madre, mucho más").[24] There is thus some sense of historical changes in women's fertility. Yerma herself equates femininity and motherhood as absolutely as the conservative doctors cited previously – when Juan tells her to act like a woman, she replies that she wishes she were one, barren as she is ("Ojalá fuera yo una mujer"; I, 2, 52). But in an echo of the "selfish" feminists who have uncoupled pleasure and procreation, the Second Girl whom Yerma encounters on her way to the fields takes pride in her own childlessness, praising the sterile free love that so alarmed both religious moralists and racial hygienists – she did not choose to marry but rather was married off (". . . me han casado"). Now only the little girls remain unwed. The Second Girl even claims that there is no reason for her husband to be her husband – they do the same now as they did when he was her boyfriend ("lo mismo hacíamos de novios que ahora"; I, 2, 48). In her scorn for the "foolishness of old folk" ("tonterías de los viejos") the challenge of modernity is heard once more.

The second girl's mother, Dolores, to whom Yerma will later appeal, offers her daughter herbal brews to make her pregnant. And Yerma's own reliance on nourishing foods (milk and lamb stew) and her constant appeal to the humors (wet and cold, hot and dry) are reminiscent of folk or archaic medicine. For example, a sixteenth-century Spanish treatise on sterility, republished in 1923, cites Galen on the noxious influence of excessive heat and damp or cold and dryness, warning would-be mothers not to drink too much cold water. It also recommends a diet of "easily digestible" foods, such as egg yolks, mutton, and soup.[25] Likewise Yerma's belief that women's blood turns poisonous if it is not used up in pregnancy ("se les vuelve veneno"; I, 1, 41) recalls the "curdling" of unsuckled milk mixed with blood, held to be responsible for a wide range of physical and psychological maladies as late as the last decade of the eighteenth century.[26]

We have seen, however, that the image repertoire of Yerma's hymns to motherhood (of swollen rivers and well-tilled fields) recurs in the more lyrical pages of conservative doctors contemporary with García Lorca. And the popular prejudices voiced by the play's characters can also be shown to have an empirical basis in the medical accounts of the period. Thus Yerma accepts, but without what Aza calls "the sweet resignation of our women,"[27] that the prospective mother is inevitably responsible for the failure to conceive. Just as the doctor claims it is "axiomatic" that sterility should not always be laid at the woman's door, even when she attributes it to herself, so in García Lorca the wise Old Pagan Woman hints, already in Act I, that Yerma should not be so innocent and that God should curse "men with rotten seed that swamps the joyful fields" ("los hombres de simiente podrida que encharcan la alegría de los campos"; I, 2, 47).

The second popular prejudice, and this time it is voiced not by Yerma but by the Old Woman, is that woman's pleasure is essential to conception. The Old Woman tells Yerma that "men have to please" – they must undo women's tresses and give them water from their own mouths ("Los hombres . . . han de deshacernos las trenzas y darnos de beber agua en su misma boca"; I, 2, 46). However, it is not Yerma's husband, Juan, but her childhood sweetheart, Víctor, who makes her "tremble." For Aza, once more, this is the main complaint of childless couples – that the woman does not conceive because "she feels no voluptuous participation in coitus."[28] Repressing women's libido (like Yerma) and uncoupling desire and conception (unlike the Old Woman), the gynecologist claims that "women's sexual pleasure is always a kind of luxury, which is not necessary for the maintenance of intellectual and physical life, nor for the reproduction of the species" (p. 14). Aza derives the "romantic prejudice" that would argue the contrary from "some of the greatest classics of our literature and the most passionate plays of contemporary theater" (p. 16). Whether or not he had García Lorca in mind (*Yerma*'s premiere had been some seven years before and García Lorca's works were, of course, no longer performed), his description of the phenomenon is eerily Lorcan – "the cry [*grito*] in the blood" that is thought to mark the coincidence of mutual desire and fertilization (p. 15). This is that very same cry of the phantom child whose suffocated voice Yerma hears when she confronts Víctor for the second time at the end of Act I ("un niño . . . lloraba como ahogado"; I, 2, 51).

The cover of Aza's *La esterilidad en la mujer* features line drawings of a white-gowned and -gloved doctor holding up a newborn child, as if displaying it to an audience, and of other smiling children delivered by a friendly stork or climbing out of a ribboned egg. No mother appears. There could be no clearer expression of both the exclusion of women effected by the medicalization of childbirth and the coexistence in Spain in the period of modern and archaic models of motherhood. I have argued that echoes of contemporary debates over feminism and reproductive rights can be glimpsed in the words of the Second Girl and the Old Woman, just as Yerma's own idealization of motherhood can be placed in the context of the potential uncoupling of desire and procreation at once effected and feared by the medical profession. As we shall see, for the biologist Marañón one menace of modernity, at once natural and monstrous, was the bi- or intersexual woman, with whom (I will argue) Yerma may be identified.

3. Marañón: Choking the One Within

In Act I, Yerma tells the Old Woman that the first time she went out with Juan she saw herself reflected in his eyes, so tiny it was as if she were her own daughter ("para verme mi chica . . . como si yo fuera hija mía"; I, 2, 46). This image of the one within (of a subject confined or imprisoned inside another) recurs throughout the play; and I shall argue that it suggests not only the subjection of women to restrictive male norms but also the incorporation of one sex into the other – Marañón's dream and nightmare of bisexuality.

In a stream of popular and clinical texts of the 1920s and 1930s, Marañón sought to reconcile the incommensurable disciplines of endocrinology, morphology, and Freudian-derived psychology. Such a project was clearly quixotic, marrying the modern chemical analysis of hormones with the archaic pseudoscience of body types, and a contemporary theory of mind that had divorced itself from its organic origins. The commentator Gary D. Keller is clearly correct in his threefold critique of Marañón's enterprise: the latter is taxonomical or descriptive, rather than explanatory; it is deterministic in its view of behavior, making no allowance for free will; and, finally, as social science it is "metaphysical," lacking "experimental controls, prior defining of theorems . . . [and] statistical or mathematical models."[29] However, it is precisely Marañón's lack of systematic rigor that is attractive to the cultural critic, rich as his texts are in productive contradictions. One of these contradictions relates, as we shall see, to his repeated assertion of universal, organic bisexuality, a "discovery" that, writing after Marañón's death, the philosopher and exegete Laín Entralgo claimed was now "universally recognized."[30] Laín is also enthusiastic about Marañón's espousal of eugenics – "daring" in 1929; generally accepted, he claims, in the Spain of the 1960s (p. 170).

Marañón's politics, before the Civil War at least, were more progressive than those of his fellow doctors whom I have cited previously – he was in favor of divorce, civil rights for women, and contraception for those who did not share his own Catholic convictions. Yet, as Geraldine Scanlon notes, his advocacy of bisexuality was cited in Parliament in an attempt to deny women suffrage; and the "scarecrow" of ambiguous sexuality stalks his texts, insisting on the necessity of educating women and men on the obligations inevitably imposed on them by their respective sexes.[31]

This curious combination of progressive politics and regressive physiology seems to apply to García Lorca also, who at the time of *Yerma*'s premiere was at once calling for a socially responsible theater and committed to traditional notions of artistic value and gender roles.[32] But Yerma's progressive loss of femininity, which culminates in the strangling of her husband and on which critics have long remarked,[33] provides a chance at least for the unsettling of sexual differences that have initially been laid down (in García Lorca, in Marañón) with such emphatic insistence.

Ever sensitive to human suffering, Marañón is dismayed by infant mortality in the Spain of the 1920s – Spanish women are poor mothers who are excessively fertile. Indeed, there is an inverse relation between a woman's number of pregnancies and the survival rate of her children.[34] Mothers accept such deaths as a "tragedy" or "act of nature" – "like the hailstorms which have destroyed a ripe harvest" (p. 49). Nothing, however, is so monstrously antinatural as this "catastrophic" loss of children, who would have lived if cared for in a "rational" way (p. 50). Marañón calls for "conscious motherhood" and for "sterile love," the hygienic and eugenic solution (pp. 52–3). It follows that couples should marry not for love but rather for economic convenience – woman should offer herself not to the man with the best-developed muscles but to the man with the "best fed flocks of sheep."[35]

Curiously, perhaps, this preference for convenience over love is held to be the result of "biological instinct." This is because in Marañón, initially at least, the biological and the social are simply the same: In his first substantial nonmedical publication, a pamphlet on "biology and feminism," Marañón argues that the metabolic constitutions of the sexes determine the social roles of each – man is "catabolic," tending toward expenditure of vital energy; woman is "anabolic," characterized by reserve.[36] History is thus abolished and the primitive human couple become a model for the modern marriage (p. 14). In a circular argument, social action is defined as a "male sexual function" from which women are, necessarily, excluded (p. 15); and motherhood and participation in society are branded "opposed sexual characteristics" (*Tres ensayos*, p. 45).

Elsewhere, however, the ravages of modernity disrupt such comforting binaries. In a lecture on "the hygiene of emotion" read to an audience of young ladies, Marañón laments the proliferation of nervous diseases caused by the frantic haste of urban life.[37] Medical advances raise the prospect of controlling affect – a female patient can be made to weep at the thought of her lost children by an injection of adrenalin (p. 12). But the sexually charged atmosphere of the city permits only one "antidote" – the flight into nature (p. 28). In another essay the abnormal convulsions of modern life are explicitly associated with female sterility. For Marañón the cult of sport is particularly noxious in both men and women. Sport, he claims, is infertility; and sport is to work as prostitution is to motherhood – the triumph of momentary pleasure over a pain required for the survival of the species (*Tres ensayos*, p. 74). True happiness, he writes, lies in a balance between "sterile delight and anguished creation."

The short-haired, sports-crazed modern woman is clearly a threat. But medicine can now achieve "theatrical" transformations in manly women – the grafting of sex glands can make "a bearded, sterile woman conceive a large number of children, at the same time imparting to her appearance and very character a clear conversion to the femininity which was once doubtful [*borrosa*]" (*Tres ensayos*, p. 190). And, in accordance with the unpredictable interaction of endocrinology and morphology, gender stereotypes are perversely unstable in Marañón – thus the passionate Carmen is the type of the "virile" woman and the seductive Don Juan that of the "feminized" man.[38] The sexually timid male, fearful of wasting his precious reserves on the fathering of children, may be more truly manly than his proudly strutting rival.[39]

It thus follows that, in spite of the primacy of sexual difference, intersexual states are ubiquitous: "Intersexuality is an element of contemporary sexual normality and a knowledge of it is one of the necessary starting points for future normality."[40] Male and female fuse just as night and day merge "in the long hours of twilight into an infinite gradation of moments" (p. 3). Following Freud, Marañón believes that woman's libido is masculine – infantile, passive, and narcissistic (p. 47). The true pleasure of her sex is thus motherhood: "The real orgasm of the normal woman is in the pleasure with which she hopes to become a mother, in the moment at which she embraces her child for the first time, and in the infinite delight she takes in the immediate duties of motherhood" (p. 53). Marañón means this quite literally – he cites a woman of "irreproachable conduct" who was "tormented" by the physical pleasure she felt when breast feeding. Indeed sexual pleasure and motherhood are mutually exclusive – another patient, excessively orgasmic, did not fall pregnant until she had had one ovary removed, thus, writes Marañón, ending her capacity for sexual pleasure (p. 234).

In spite of this idealization of motherhood, however, and in spite of Marañón's evolutionism (which has him claim that inter-sexual types are increasingly rare), the manly woman is the object of praise, representing as she does "a superior modality of her sex" (p. 171). Moreover, Marañón insists repeatedly that, because of biological bisexuality, each of us carries within us the trace of the other sex. Thus the early essay on biology and feminism states:

Sexual inversion . . . is not monstrous, but a frequent and natural phe-nomenon within its own abnormality. . . . The most masculine men bear hidden within them female seeds [*gérmenes*] that are muffled or dimmed [*amortiguados*]; and the most feminine women also carry potential traces of the male, sleeping deep inside them [*en sus en-trañas*]. (*Biología y feminismo*, p. 38)

Marañón calls this tendency "partial heterosexualism"; that is, "incorporation of the other sex." In the three essays on sexuality he is yet more graphic:

We cannot free ourselves of the presence of a representation of the other sex which today we know accompanies us, infiltrated into our very being, and, like an invisible sprite [*duende*], sets traps at every step for our rightly inclined instinct. Each man . . . carries a phantom woman within him, not in the imagination, for then it would be easily expelled, but circulating in the blood; and each woman also bears a more or less substantial phantom man. And that woman or man traced within us [*en esbozo*], not those which are made of flesh and blood, are the ones which lead us into pain and sin. This . . . is a vital discovery of modern science. (*Tres ensayos*, p. 167)

What are we to do with these troublingly persistent imagos? Marañón is vehement – men and women must "suffocate" the re-mainders of the other sex (p. 180). And he ends with a ringing, but puzzling, invocation to Spanish youth: "Kill the phantom of the other sex which each of you bears within; be men, be women, and then the women and men who walk the world will be no more to you than fonts of chastity" (p. 213).

What did Marañón make of *Yerma*, then, on its premiere? No doubt he agreed with the main theme – that a woman's true plea-sure lies not in sex but in motherhood. He may well have disapproved of the Old Woman of Act I, a paradigm of "unconscious motherhood," whose fertility is matched only by the fatal destiny of her children – six out of fourteen failed to survive ("catorce hijos, seis murieron"; I, 2, 44). Marañón's belief in marriage of convenience is echoed by Juan, constantly citing his well-fed flocks as proof that Yerma should be happy. And the archaic social divisions of the village reproduce the sexual oppositions Marañón believes to be fundamental to human life: Juan states that women should remain at home, like sheep in the pen ("Las ovejas en el redil y las mujeres en su casa"; II, 2, 63); Yerma claims that men have a social life, whereas women have no function but childbirth and child care ("las mujeres no tenemos más que esta [vida] de la cría y el cuido de la cría"; II, 2, 64). Yerma's village could thus be seen as García Lorca's response to the "flight into nature" recommended by Marañón.

Marañón's equation of pleasure and sterility is echoed by the washerwomen, who complain that childless women run wild in the street and are soft and pampered creatures, fearful of stretch marks ("el vientre arrugado"; II, 1, 55). Yerma may be far from the short-haired, sporty flappers of the city, but her infertility marks her, like them, as a potential prostitute to her neighbors, however firmly she embraces motherhood as woman's only true libido and pain as the source of happiness.

Moreover, the washerwomen brand Yerma a "machorra" – at once a sterile cow and a virilized woman. Yerma herself suggests her own intersexual state to María, claiming that she will end up believing that she is her own son. When, sleepless, she goes at night to feed the oxen (a task never before undertaken by a woman), her steps resound like those of a man ("mis pasos me suenan a pasos de hombre"; II, 2, 67). Of course, there can be no prospect here of a "theatrical" transformation through the surgical intervention Marañón promises virilized women. And in this twilight zone of sexual difference, love and maternal desire can be reread as a fantastically visceral incorporation of the other sex within: Yerma "carries" Víctor with her, "represented in her eyes" ("retratado en los ojos"; II, 1, 56); her belly bears within it "tender children" or perhaps "sons" ("tiernos hijos"; II, 2, 66).

Inversely, Juan plays the part of the "timid" man, hoarding precious resources he dare not expend on unproductive children (II, 2, 62) and lacking in the "will" ("voluntad") to control his virilized wife (II, 2, 64). This is a new model of masculinity, little appreciated in García Lorca's rural setting, however appropriate it might be for Marañón's frenetically sex-charged metropolis. There is thus a sense of the fragility of male sexual development in García Lorca that is confirmed by the vehemence and compulsive reiteration of Marañón's calls for Spanish youth to assume their sexual destiny.

Moreover, Marañón's image of the "heterosexual" remainder confined within the very body of the desiring subject might lead us to a new reading of the theme of silence in Act II. Yerma keeps her suffering "stuck close to her flesh," defiantly refusing to speak ("pegado a mis carnes"; II, 2, 63); and she tells Víctor as he leaves that "there are things enclosed within walls, unspoken, . . . which, if they burst out and shouted, would fill the world" ("Hay cosas encerradas detrás de los muros . . . que si salieran de pronto y gritaran, llenarían el mundo"; II, 2, 70). These lines cannot refer to her childlessness, which is apparent to all, and appear to allude to the love for Víctor that the code of honor Yerma has internalized forbids her to acknowledge. However, Marañón's doctrine of bisexuality ("a vital discovery of modern science") is a more potent example of that hidden truth whose revelation would transform social and sexual life as a whole. This is not to argue, as previous critics have, however, that García Lorca identified in his homosexuality with Yerma in her infertility.[41] It is, rather, to suggest that in the medical imaginary of the period the invert man and the sterile woman are twin types of intersexuality ("normal in their abnormality"), both of whom take up their position at the limits of sexual difference, where day shades, imperceptibly, into night.

Marañón wrote, sympathetically for his time, of what he called the "tragedy" of sexual inversion:

Beyond the obvious pervert there extends a great circle of human beings who bear in silence the tragedy of their sexual disorder. I have heard in my surgery the most unexpected confessions from people who never awoke the slightest suspicion of their twisted instincts even in their most intimate acquaintances. I shall never forget . . . the stammering confession of a man full of intelligence and goodness, whose life was a model of correct behavior, and who I did not see again until years later when I came across his corpse on the mortuary slab [after his suicide]. (*Tres ensayos*, p. 185)

In a footnote Marañón thanks the numerous inverts who have corresponded with him, claiming that they are perhaps the greatest of heroes, for their heroism is wholly invisible and can have no moment of "theatrical glamour" ("resplandor teatral"; p. 235, n. 65).

Timid heroes of the sexual struggle, inverts are the brothers of the virilized woman, Yerma. While the former struggle to suffocate the feminine phantoms that they (like all men) bear within them, Yerma will turn repression into aggression, strangling the other sex whom she too carries deep inside her, the man who is also, according to her final, anguished cry, her own son. The darkness in which Act II ends, a darkness in which Yerma's name is spoken for the first time in the play, is thus symptomatic of that intersexual state, which remained in García Lorca's time as ubiquitous as it was mysterious.

4. Anxiety, Hysteria, Bisexuality

Cipriano Rivas Cherif, a well-known director in the Spain of the 1930s, left a testimony of García Lorca's attitude to Freud just after the premiere of *Yerma* in 1935. Rivas claims that García Lorca told him he attributed his "frigidity" toward women to infantile memories of his mother's too-close attentions – she would leap from her bed to his cot to comfort him if he awoke in the night.[42] When Rivas replies that García Lorca did not remember it but rather read it in Freud, the two friends share a laugh of complicity with each other.

As we shall see, Laín Entralgo also claims that Freud was well known to those who flocked to the first production of *Yerma*. Rivas's anecdote, however, suggests a model for a psychoanalytic approach to García Lorca – one that shares the playwright's keen interest in Freud but preserves a certain ironic skepticism and sympathetic humor.

Less is known of García Lorca's approach to Freud than of Marañón's, which is based on criteria at once nationalist, biologist, and moralizing. Thus, first, Marañón claims that Freud's discoveries are not appropriate for southern or Mediterranean societies, and that Freud's "normality" is peculiar to northern or central Europe, or perhaps to the analyst's own "race." Second, he claims that Freud pays too little attention to neurological or physiological conditions and is ignorant of biological law. Finally, he finds psychoanalysis intrusive and voyeuristic – the specialist should enter man's soul quietly and reverently as if in a library, and rather than "disturb" the unconscious, he should bury it still further.[43]

What I shall argue, however, is that far from neglecting the physiological, Freud is concerned precisely with the interaction between the somatic and the psychic. And the evolution of this relation can be traced in his varied accounts of two categories vital to Yerma's anamnesis – anxiety and bisexuality. Unlike Marañón's versions of eugenics and intersexuality, Freud's terms are more productive and less pathologizing even at the most literal level of his text. Yet both terms are unstable. Anxiety precipitates a series of increasingly fine distinctions (between neurosis and hysteria, actual and psychic, present and past). Freud's successive revisions trace psychoanalysis's turn toward fantasy as a motive of repression, even as it holds true to the demands of the real. Bisexuality, meanwhile, is a "difficulty" for Freud[44] (as it is for Marañón) that also shifts from an organic to a psychic frame of reference, as Freud gradually theorizes more subtle models of repression, identification, and aggression. What these terms offer *Yerma* is thus the possibility of a reading that is neither simply historicist (like that of the conservative doctors) nor brutally biologist (like that of Marañón) but rather takes sexuality as a mediator between external and internal, between experience and constitution. Such an understanding may shed light on some notorious obscurities in García Lorca's last act.

Already in 1895 Freud sought to separate the newly named anxiety neurosis from the traditional neurasthenia, or nervous debility.[45] Freud offers a symptomatology of the former – irritability, auditory hyperaesthesia, anxious expectation, and excessive moral scrupulousness (pp. 37–8). Disturbance of bodily functions includes spasms of the heart, difficulty in breathing, shivering, vertigo, and congestions (pp. 39–40). The etiology of anxiety neurosis is sexual, affecting as it does "women whose husbands suffer . . . from markedly impaired potency" (p. 46). But its novelty and differentiation from hysteria lie in its imperviousness to psychotherapy – this is because it is not motivated by repression and does not exhibit mechanisms of substitution or conversion (pp. 43–4). Lacking a psychical origin, it is but a "deflection of somatic sexual excitation from the physical sphere and . . . a consequent abnormal employment of that excitation" (p. 55). As such, this "alienation between the somatic and the psychic" might easily be confused with what Freud calls the "artificial [i.e., socially enforced] retarding of the female sexual instinct" (p. 56).

An essay of 1905 on the etiology of neuroses[46] elaborates upon this original distinction between the physically unmediated and the psychically elaborated, distinguishing between "actual" neuroses, whose etiology is contemporary, and psychoneuroses, whose origins lie in the remote past (pp. 74, 80). But Freud now claims, famously, that infantile memories of seduction are more commonly fantasies; and moreover, no experience can be pathogenic unless it has first been repressed (p. 77). The normal and the neurotic differ only in the degree of that repression, and "neurotic illnesses cannot be sharply differentiated from health" (p. 81). Freud gestures toward endocrinology here, stating that "the processes which determine the formation and utilization of sexual libido . . . are in the last resort of a chemical nature" (p. 80).

As Freud elaborates upon the twin notions of the unconscious and repression, he thus also allows for a certain mode of conscious and contemporary psychic action.[47] Thus in daydreams, "invariably erotic" in women (p. 86), it may be possible for "unconscious fantasy to be captured in consciousness" (p. 88). Freud's example here is of a childless woman who fantasized that she had been abandoned by the imaginary lover who had fathered her dream child –

bursting into tears, she suddenly became aware of her fantasy. Freud continues that there are hysterics who do not express their fantasies as symptoms but rather as "conscious realizations, and in that way they devise and stage assaults, attacks, or acts of sexual aggression" (p. 90). Such fantasies commonly combine a "simultaneity of contradictory actions"; and their highest degree of complexity is when they are bisexual (pp. 93–4). Just as when masturbating a man may consciously identify with both male and female partners in a sexual act, so in a hysterical attack a woman "plays both parts," both pressing her dress up against her body and attempting to tear it off. The "innate bisexual disposition in man" is thus most clearly visible in psychoneurotics, who take advantage of the "convenient possibility of constantly switching . . . as though on to an adjoining track" (p. 94).

It is no surprise that an almost contemporary paper on hysterical attacks[48] should also stress theatricality and bisexual identification – an attack is a fantasy "portrayed in pantomime"; and a revival of infantile sexuality which is of "an essentially masculine character" (p. 102). Hysterical neurosis is thus a consequent of that "wave of repression which, by doing away with her masculine sexuality, allows the woman to emerge." The language clearly anticipates Marañón's appeal to women to suffocate the man within; but here it takes up its place within an increasingly elaborate and theorized account of the psychic economy and its relation to the body.

A case history of a woman unable to have children illustrates this attempt to reconcile the inner world and the demands of reality.[49] Freud does not take the patient's desire to conceive for granted; rather it is based in this case on "an infantile fixation of her wishes" (p. 137). Aware of her unhappiness and unconscious reproach, her sterile husband begins to "fail in sexual intercourse" (p. 138). The wife falls into an obsessional neurosis that is anal and sadistic in character, regressing to a time when "the primacy of genital zones [was] not yet established" (p. 139), both "reactivating her [primordial] masculine sexuality" and mounting "a defensive struggle against it" (p. 144). Addressing "biological" lines of thought, Freud claims that such neuroses cannot be reduced to the "antithesis between male and female" and "the reproductive function" (p. 140) – for to hold that "sexual life coincides with the genital and reproductive function . . . would place us outside psychoanalysis" (p. 141).

The role of bisexuality in the destabilizing of sexual oppositions recurs in the famous "A Child Is Being Beaten" of 1919.[50] In masochistic fantasy the female child "escapes from the demands of her erotic life [and] turns herself . . . into a man" (p. 187). Now "a spectator of the event which takes the place of a sexual act" (p. 187), she causes boys to be beaten "since she has become a boy" (p. 188). In the second half of this essay Freud refutes two theories of bisexuality, biological and sociological respectively. The first is that of Fliess, who sees a "struggle between two sexual characters" (p. 188) caused by a common bisexual constitution – "with men, what is unconscious and repressed [is] feminine instinctual impulses; and conversely with women" (p. 189). Freud rejects this, just as he rejects the genital and reproductive explanation of neurosis: "Such a theory . . . can only have an intelligible meaning if we assume that a person's sex is determined by the formation of his genitals." The second theory is that of Adler, who sees the "masculine protest" as proof that all human beings "desire to break away from the feminine line," aspiring to the "superior" male sex (p. 189). For Freud, this neglects the flexible resources of repression – "both in male and female individuals masculine as well as feminine instinctual impulses are found, and each can equally well undergo repression and become unconscious" (pp. 190–1). Just as sex cannot be reproduced to reproduction, so repression cannot be made to divide along simple sexual lines.

Those simple lines are also blurred by Yerma in Act III. Thus, as the curtain rises, the wise woman Dolores compliments Yerma on her fearlessness during the (unseen) fertility ritual in the graveyard: Yerma is the only woman to be unafraid in such circumstances ("todas han pasado miedo . . . menos tú"; III, 1, 73). Virilized by her valor, still Yerma is frankly sexual in her continued appetite for motherhood – claiming she would lick her newborn clean like a beast and rhapsodizing over the swelling of her breasts with streams of milk ("ese arroyo de leche tibia que les va llenando los pechos"; III, 1, 74). Yet she also exhibits that "dissociation from the external world" that Freud calls psychotic (p. 215) – claiming that, childless as she is, men and objects seem insubstantial to her, as if they were made of cotton wool ("cosas de algodón"). Indulging in masochistic daydreams, she declares that she would welcome a son even if he were to "torture" ("martirizar") her. In an echo of Marañón she claims that it is better to be knifed by a real man than to grieve over the "phantom" ("fantasma") whom she bears within.

Yerma's *idée fixe* coincides with the symptomatology of anxiety neurosis – already she has complained of the disturbance of bodily functions and senses, such as when she hears the choked cry of the child ("auditory hyperaesthesia"). And anxious expectation (Freud's "nuclear symptom") defines her existence. Now she displays the moral overscrupulousness that is, for Freud, also typically neurotic – rejecting Juan's claim that she has been with another man, vehemently maintaining her "decency" (III, 1, 77). Insensitive to sexual pleasure (in Freud's word, "anaesthetic"), Yerma is disgusted by hot-blooded women; and her circumstances mime the etiology of anxiety neurosis – the coolly inadequate husband who simply "covers" ("cubre") her when making love and who now reproaches her for her dissatisfaction.

Yet if we take the cause of Yerma's complaint to be sexual, still her condition might remain inaccessible to psychotherapy and lacking in a psychic origin – a diagnosis of anxiety neurosis would mean that somatic sexual excitation had simply been deflected from its normal employment. Its cause would be her current ("actual") excessive repression, different only in degree from that of a normal person; and her distress could not be attributed, as in hysteria, to repressed fantasies from the remote past. Yet, as Yerma enters "the darkest part of the well" ("lo más oscuro del pozo"; III, 1, 79), she herself draws a distinction between the psychic and the somatic, conscious and unconscious – it is, she says, one thing to want something with one's head and quite another for the body to respond in kind. And in her rejection of Juan's jealous recriminations, she gives voice to a sexual daydream, masochistic once more, whose value she does not capture into consciousness – if he can smell another man on her, she would have Juan strip her naked in the square and spit on her ("Me pones desnuda en la mitad de la plaza y me escupes"; III, 1, 77).

Hence if we do read Yerma's behavior as hysterical conversion (and thus run the risk of pathologizing her), then we must see her symptoms as embodying Freud's highest level of complexity: bisexuality. Thus in the final and most abstracted location (the hermitage high in the mountains), Yerma sings of the ambiguous figure of a Christ or an angel, flowing with milk and opening like a rose ("arroyos de leche . . . abre tu rosal"; III, 2, 82). And the staging of the scene that follows, when girls enter with multicolored ribbons to a crescendo of voices and bells, suggests a conversion of that overload of excitation which is the basis of hysterical attack. Music and dance signal here, as elsewhere, the "pantomime" of libidinal economy. But the overt theatricality of the "male" and "female" masks in their fertility ritual need not signal, as it might first appear, a return to simple sexual difference and genital reproduction. For just as in fantasy the patient may identify alternately with the male and female positions, so in their song the masks switch tracks between first, second, and third persons – thus the Female laments the lot of the "sad wife" ("la esposa triste") bathing in the river and then predicts that she (in the first person) will tear her petticoats when night comes; or again the Male addresses the wife in the second person, boasts of his potency in the first, and then praises the couple's multiple couplings in the third (III, 2, 83–5). Yerma may stand by like the masochistic girl child, "a spectator of the event which takes the place of a sexual act." But as in the fluid identifications of neurotic fantasy, primacy has not been established, and sexual life is gloriously, shamelessly excessive.

The Old Woman from the first act attempts to cure Yerma by offering her a solution in the real – she should come to live with her son, because Juan's infertility is constitutional, inherited from his sickly forefathers (III, 2, 87). Angrily declining the offer, Yerma gives the puzzling response that her "suffering is no longer in [her] flesh" ("dolor que ya no está en las carnes"; III, 2, 88). Here she hints at the primacy of the psychic over what was once somatic. Just as Freud rejects the two mechanistic theories of bisexuality in favor of a more subtle understanding of the coexistence of contradictory forces within the subject, so Yerma rejects simply material solutions to her quandary – first the Old Woman's offer of a substitute lover; second, and finally, Juan's offer of a sterile love, a kiss that bears no promise of children within it (III, 2, 90). For Yerma (as for Freud) sex cannot simply be reduced to reproduction (outside marriage, children have no value); but neither can the real, for all the urgency of its demands, substitute for the psychic need that has now outstripped it: Juan's proposal that she settle, as he has, for what "[he] hold[s] in [his] hands, sees through [his] eyes" ("lo que tengo entre las manos, lo que veo por los ojos"; III, 2, 89) is met with horror. If Yerma's effortless killing of her husband is thus a "masculine protest," a final manifestation of that libido which is for Freud and Marañón always masculine and which deserves to be repressed or suffocated, then it is also a disavowal, albeit psychotic, of an external world that neglects the psyche and of a sex reduced to the tyranny of the genital organs and reproductive functions: Yerma has finally killed her child.

5. Between Blood and Sex

On 29 November 1971 a controversial production of *Yerma* opened at the Teatro de la Comedia in Madrid. Directed by Víctor García and starring Nuria Espert, the play was staged on a canvas stretched taut across the acting space – womblike, the canvas also served as a flexible floor, a sheltering roof or tent, and a billowing sail. As in 1935, reactions were mixed, often dividing along political lines. Thus Alfredo Marquerie in *El Pueblo* claims that "part of the audience was left stupefied," while the rest (the youthful contingent) burst into cheers as García greeted them "with strange gestures" and the actors turned somersaults on the trampoline-set.[51] The publicity shot for this review shows Espert off stage – glaring out from behind disheveled hair, ferocious in a leopardskin coat.

As in 1935, then, the Right complained both of the "obscenity" of the production (*El Pueblo* cites "half naked women") and of the frighteningly unfamiliar audience. But García was also attacked from the left: Enrique Romero in *Triunfo* claimed that García Lorca's text is concerned with the "alienation" of women subject to the power of their proprietor-husbands, and that the solution it proposes is "revolutionary" – by the end of the work Yerma has "liberated" herself, although she remains unaware of her own "contradictions."[52] For *Triunfo* the "formalism" of the production (its reliance on a performing star, Espert; its appeal to "gratuitous" sound and lighting effects) distracts from García Lorca's revolutionary content and the social "commitment" proper to theater – this production is directed only to the fashionably progressive *petit bourgeois* who will ensure its commercial success.

Critics of all political persuasions agree that García Lorca's text is overwhelmed by the visual brilliance (or impertinence) of the staging – in this "director's theater," image takes precedence over word.[53] I argue that this bias is experienced, like anxiety neurosis, as dangerously regressive – the production uses formally primitive means of representation directly to express a somatic excitation that has not been psychically or intellectually worked over. However, it is the extreme right *El Alcázar* that vindicates this "interesting experiment against the Lorcan clichés" – while those who remember the "unforgettable" Margarita Xirgu in 1935 will be disappointed, that "tradition" has now dwindled into "outdated folklore."[54] The experimental staging is thus "questionable," but still "admissible."

Laín Entralgo, Marañón's exegete and another theatergoer who remembers the 1935 production, devotes two pieces to the 1971 production in the weekly *Gaceta Ilustrada*. In the first he argues, like other critics, that there is a now twin audience for *Yerma* – the nostalgists, who long for a time in which text was sacrosanct, and the experimentalists, who revel in technical innovation.[55] Both of these groups claim to enlist Federico's support for their approach. Yet Laín adds an interesting historical note to the Margarita Xirgu production, claiming that the original audience was full of "neo-Malthusians" (the phrase is familiar from the 1930s) controlling their own fertility who, nonetheless, enthusiastically applauded a play in which marital sterility was depicted as a tragedy. In the second piece Laín adds that "Freudianism" had also gained general approval at that time.[56] However, a social and intellectual change has intervened in the years since García Lorca's death, a change that may be attributed to the increasing awareness of Freud's account of the libido – now it is not infertility but sexual frustration that obsesses society. This, then, is the achievement of Nuria Espert and Víctor García – they focus on the latter theme while allowing others to appear in the background "as if they were old and faded daguerreotypes." The "resurrection" of *Yerma* thus lies in the superimposition of historical meanings achieved by the very contemporary talent of the "universal and quintessentially Catalan" Espert.

It seems unlikely that García and Espert were actively seeking the approval of Catholic philosophers and members of the Royal Academy such as Laín when they mounted their experimental production. And the avant-garde theater out of which their *Yerma* had grown, which stressed physical mime over well-spoken text, would be progressively "domesticated" in the transition to democracy that was already beginning.[57] Outside Spain also, once-transgressive topics or interpretations of García Lorca have since been rendered commonplace, neutralized – a London fringe production of 1995, otherwise traditional, even folkloric, implies a homosexual relationship between Juan and Víctor.[58] Once more the vulgarization of Freud (in this case the "reversal of affect" in jealousy)[59] permits new readings of the play that (like faded photographs) do not simply obscure the original text but are rather superimposed on it, permitting previous meanings to persist and to make their presence felt.

In his introduction to Marañón's three essays on sexuality, Pérez de Ayala writes that the old Spanish conventional morality is like a whitened sepulcher – immaculate outside, putrefied within.[60] What the modern world demands, he continues, is that we speak the truth about our lives, without hypocritical concealment (p. 21). We have seen that García Lorca also has Yerma speak of things that are kept inside but would transform the world if they were released. The cult of confession, however, so central to psychoanalysis, has of course been the object of critique by Foucault. If in Foucault the hysteric and homosexual remain linked it is because, unlike in Marañón and Freud, they are twin inventions of that medical discipline which claims, modestly, to describe them. Foucault has some well-chosen words on hysteria as a "theater of ritual crises" in the clinic of Freud's predecessor Charcot, words that are pertinent to *Yerma*.[61] But more particularly Foucault perceives a shift from archaic to modern social structures in the change from a symbolics of blood to an analytics of sexuality:

Nothing was more on the side of of the law, death, transgression, the symbolic, and sovereignty than blood; just as sexuality was on the side of the norm, knowledge, life, meaning, the disciplines, and regulations. (p. 148)

I argue, finally, that *Yerma* the play and Yerma the character are placed on the cusp of these two organizational principles – the first marking the florid spectacle of heredity and ritual (the blood line), the second the disciplinary drama of surveillance and the psyche (the sexual fix). If anxiety and bisexuality thus offer no simple answers to the problems of interpretation I posed at the beginning of this chapter, the historical context I have provided points the way forward to an anomalous figure, inconceivable to Yerma and unanticipated by the male practitioners and theorists I have cited here – the desiring mother who can fuse the maternity and sexuality that were separated for so long, bringing together blood and sex. She is the woman who will wrest reproductive technology from the hands of the professionals and whose social activities and libido will no longer be conceived of as essentially masculine in character, whether that masculinity is held to be somatic (as in Marañón) or psychic (as in Freud). Caught no more between the biology of reproduction and the medicine of sex, free at last from the simultaneous, contradictory actions of the hysteric and the oral sadistic impulses of the neurotic, truly this modern woman was to be a monstrous or a miraculous birth.

2

Black Wedding
García Lorca, Langston Hughes, and the
Translation of Introjection

1. Language, Reference, Genre

The three perennial concerns of critics of *Bodas de sangre* (*Blood Wedding*), the first play in García Lorca's so-called rural trilogy, are language, reference, and genre. First, the shift from the relatively literal language of Act I to the overtly lyrical diction of Act III is sometimes seen as problematic.[1] Second, the localism and particularity of the supposed basis of *Bodas de sangre* (newspaper reports of a real-life rural drama in Níjar, Almería) contrast with the universal dimensions generally attributed to García Lorca's poetic tragedy.[2] Finally, the genre of the play is disputed – some critics have attempted, with little success, to relate García Lorca's drama to Aristotelian norms of tragedy;[3] others have proclaimed his "practice without theory" to be irreducible to standard definitions of the genre.[4] Moreover, if the problem of reference raises wider questions of regionalism and political engagement, that of tragedy also raises broader issues of prophecy and fatality, inseparable from the cult of García Lorca himself as author.

In this second chapter I approach these familiar questions of language, reference, and genre from a series of oblique angles. The first is the New York City production of *Bodas de sangre* as "Bitter Oleander" in the translation of José Weissberger in 1935, which remains unpublished and unstudied by critics.[5] Using archival documents to set this production in the context of Broadway in the period, I contrast it with Langston Hughes's translation (as "Fate at the Wedding"), unstaged until 1992 and unpublished until 1994, which reveals significant variants in emphasis and has, to my knowledge, never been examined by Lorca scholars.[6] While the responses

44

of U.S. newspaper critics to this the earliest production of García Lorca's drama in their country still frame Anglo-American critical responses, the evidence of Hughes's translation points to a far more sophisticated and empathetic understanding of García Lorca's project, one that, I argue, focuses on the male body as lost object.

As poet and dramatist, Hughes not only reveals a long-lasting interest in García Lorca[7] but also shares deeper concerns with the Spaniard: a sophisticated engagement with popular language, especially with regard to musicality and folk idiom; a passionate commitment to social equality coupled with an unwillingness to toe a party line;[8] a discreet approach to sexuality, both his own and others', one that his estate has jealously sought to defend.[9] Moreover, the cast and settings of much of Hughes's lyric (with its frequent references to gypsies and sailors, to rivers and moons) are also reminiscent, in a very different context, of García Lorca's poetry.[10] It is well known that García Lorca embraced black theater in Harlem, praising in a letter to his parents its appeal to gesture, voice, and laughter, prophesying even that black musical theater would wholly replace the white.[11] Ironically, this was a stress on gestural physicality and mime that would prove to be characteristic of New York critics' response to *Bodas de sangre* and of the production history of the Neighborhood Playhouse, the company that performed the play. Critics have paid considerable attention to García Lorca's depiction of African Americans in *Poeta en Nueva York* (*Poet in New York*).[12] In this chapter I ask, in a gesture of symbolic exchange, not what García Lorca thought of blacks but what one gifted black contemporary thought of García Lorca. Hughes's translation of *Bodas de sangre* and his own "poetic tragedy" *Mulatto,* staged on Broadway in the same year as *Bodas de sangre,* stand as an exemplary response to and intertext for García Lorca's lyrical drama.

A recent critic has spoken of the "sacrifice of manhood" in *Bodas de sangre.*[13] In this chapter I argue, beyond the inversion of gender roles suggested by that critic, for a reading of the play informed by Hughes's translation and focusing on eroticized forms of mourning, melancholia, and masochism. While Freud's accounts of these phenomena correspond to some extent to the characters depicted within García Lorca's play (with its grieving mother and suffering lovers), I argue for an economy of pleasure and unpleasure (a rhythm or temporal sequences of rises and falls of stimulus) that marks and structures the dramatic action as a whole.[14] If melancholy acts, as Freud suggests, like "a painful wound" (p. 268), it is one that underwrites the contract between text, playwright, and audience and cannot be confined to any single element of the dramatic process.

Briefly to anticipate, the mechanism at work here (within the text, within the theater) is one of incorporation or introjection, defined by Laplanche and Pontalis as, respectively: "the process whereby the subject, more or less on the level of fantasy, has an object penetrate his body and keeps it 'inside' his body"; and "[a] process revealed by analytic investigation: in fantasy, the subject transposes objects and their inherent qualities from the 'outside' to the 'inside' of himself."[15] As we shall see, these processes are linked in complex and quite specific ways to mourning, melancholia, and masochism. More generally, however, the fear of and the desire for internal cleavage or splitting and for external fusion or merger underlie the sometimes xenophobic and racist U.S. responses to *Bodas de sangre* and (more blatantly) *Mulatto,* just as they underscore the dramatic mechanism in both plays: *Mulatto* charts the demand for social incorporation by a mixed-race youth, excluded from the white body politic; *Bodas de sangre* charts the lovers' longing for merger and the final penetration of two men's bodies by the knives with which they are identified. Both plays climax with an impossible struggle to break through a circle of men (lynching party, fatal posse) that must end in death for the male subject. But, as I argue toward the end of this chapter, the fatality that runs through *Bodas de sangre* does not prevent our forging a social reading of it, one that is, nonetheless, consistent with a libidinal economy and suffused with the erotic charge that is the play's most powerful characteristic.

2. New York, 1935

Brooks Atkinson, the feared *New York Times* reviewer of both *Bodas de sangre* and *Mulatto,* was later to chart the decline of Broadway in the 1930s, when great theaters were closed, torn down, or transformed into grind houses (dubious second-run cinemas) or burlesque shows.[16] Nineteen-thirty-five was the best year in the slow recovery that followed the Crash of 1929, with the commercial houses offering historical drama (Helen Hayes in *Victoria Regina*), melodrama (Leslie Howard in *The Petrified Forest*), and musical review (Fanny Brice as Baby Snooks in *The Ziegfeld Follies*).[17] The mid-thirties also saw *agitprop*, most famously in Clifford Odets's *Waiting for Lefty*, whose celebrated final call for revolutionary sacrifice (for blood, death, and bodies in pieces) fortuitously coincides with the Lorcan image repertoire.[18] The radical agenda embraced race, with *New Theatre* of July 1935 appearing as a "Negro Number," which included a sardonic piece by Langston Hughes on the all-black heavenly musical *Green Pastures*.[19]

Bodas de sangre was staged at the Lyceum Theater, just east of Broadway on 45th Street, by the Neighborhood Playhouse. The Lyceum, physically slightly isolated from the mass of theaters crowding Times Square, had been known since its inception in 1903 for high-quality productions that attracted a loyal audience. However, its owner, David Frohman (who lived, as was customary, on site), was threatened with eviction during the Depression, and the theater was later rescued from demolition in 1939.[20] The Neighborhood Playhouse's career had been equally precarious. Founded by the Jewish philanthropists and sisters Irene and Alice Lewisohn in the far reaches of the lower East Side (Grand Street), it had since lost its permanent base: *Bodas de sangre* was, however, to mark the Playhouse company's twentieth anniversary. In his introduction to Alice Lewisohn Crowley's history of the Playhouse, Joseph Wood Krutch places it within the contemporary context of New York "little theaters."[21] While others were devoted to dramatic literature, whether politically radical or artistically sophisticated, the Playhouse was concerned with "song and dance and ritual as direct expressions of the beauty of life." This sense of physicality (of the primacy of music and movement over text) was reinforced by a certain self-conscious exoticism – the best-known productions on Grand Street were versions of the Indian epic *The Little Clay Cart* and the Jewish folk tale *The Dybbuk*. The Lewisohns' concern was almost ethnographic; they sent emissaries to Spain to gather "authentic" material for the staging of *Bodas de sangre*.[22]

The placing of *Bodas de sangre* in the theatrical geography of Manhattan is thus clear – with the Lyceum known for "quality" programming and the Neighborhood Playhouse for worthy exoticism, *Bodas de sangre* would arouse quite specific expectations even before it opened. These expectations were confirmed by the mixed responses of critics. Brooks Atkinson's review (*New York Times*, 12 February 1935) is headed "Bitter Oleander to celebrate the founding of the Neighborhood Playhouse." Beginning by citing the "twentieth anniversary of the Playhouse" ("the unworldly little theater in Grand St. where the drama was once served unselfishly and well"), he goes on to lament the current production of "a peasant play from the Spanish":

But, alas, it is twenty years since the Neighborhood Playhouse was founded and seven or eight years since it ceased its highminded activities on the East Side. The magic has gone. Lorca's drama may have something of the poetry of Spanish peasantry among the songs and simples [*sic*] of its speech. But the production is so fretted with studio attitude and so consciously formalized that nothing comes out of it. It has been removed from the soil and clapped in the straitjacket of style.

In the *New York World Telegram* of the same date ("Bitter Oleander on view at Lyceum"), the debonair, mustachioed Robert Garland combined an anti-Semitic jibe at translator José Weissberger ("he's not so spick and Spanish, either") with a somewhat similar placing of the production in New York theatrical geography, claiming that "these adaptations from the Spanish [should not] be exposed to the biting winds of Broadway": "[*Bodas de sangre*] is not at ease in the Lyceum, where the delectable odor of [comedy] *Sailor, Beware* remains. Instead it is self-conscious, arty, what is spoken of as 'little theater.'" Inevitably, *Bodas de sangre* on Broadway becomes inseparable from U.S. dramatic conflicts – artistic versus commercial, downtown versus midtown, highbrow versus hedonistic.

Hostile accounts tend to focus on language. In "Flowers of

Spain," the *New York Sun* of 16 February begins by enumerating the horticultural motifs of the dialogue:

A deceased gentleman is lovingly remembered by his widow not only as "my carnation," but also as one of her "two geraniums." Her dead son was the other geranium. A mother looks affectionately on her sleeping baby and breathes: "My little rose-bush."

Hyman Goldberg ("The Reporter at the Play") narrates in the *New York Evening Post* of 12 February a dispute in the audience as to whether an oleander is a flower, a tree, or a Spanish onion. This lighthearted piece offers valuable evidence of audience responses – one woman is clearly bohemian ("with a wrap that looked like a crazy quilt"); a "strikingly beautiful brunette" pronounces the play "altogether outdated" and not for "these enlightened days"; a businessman from Jackson Heights claims, "I've read the play by Lorca in Spanish. It's a good translation and the actors are doing a good job of portraying the people." New York audiences may not have been quite so ignorant of Spanish drama as recent Spanish scholars seem to believe – most press reviews compare Lorca to his compatriot Jacinto Benavente, one of whose plays had opened on Broadway the week before.

If *Bodas de sangre*'s language is held to be affected, then it is consistent with the play's presumed referent: Spain or, more particularly, Andalusia. The supposed exaggerations of the region are caught in the title of one review: "Andalusians of Grandeur" (12 February). Here John Mason Brown claims that the "torrid melodrama . . . seems fated to do little more to American audiences than remind them of the size of the wide Atlantic." . . . "[García Lorca's] people," he continues, "are great ones for talking as if they had eaten whole libraries full of seed catalogues."[23] The play is "verbal gardening." Significantly, more sympathetic critics focus on the genre of the play. Henry Senber's "Bitter Oleander excels as poetic drama" in the *New York Telegraph* of 13 February misspells the playwright's name as "Lorco" but praises the "feeling for poetic tragedy" displayed by Nance O'Neil as the mother (Figure 1) and the "smooth, flowing gestures" of Eugenie Leontovich as the bride.

Figure 1. Nance O'Neil (Mother) in *Bodas de sangre* (*Bitter Oleander/ Blood Wedding*), New York 1935.

In general, then, New York critics found *Bodas de sangre*'s language florid, its theme exotic, and its tragic fatality outdated and unmodern. These prejudices still hold true today in many Anglo-American responses to Lorca. Critics of the 1930s expressed their resistance in images of unhappy introjection – the swallowing of seed catalogues or onions. But if this refusal of merger was influenced by the play's production history, it may have been overdetermined by the performance history and styles of the actors, mentioned in the last review. Nance O'Neil (whose scrapbooks preserve the mixed notices I cite here) had gone from tragic lover (*Camille*, 1900; *Hedda Gabler*, 1904) to Biblical heroine (*The Wanderer*, 1917). Her greatest success had been with another Spanish play – Benavente's *The Passion Flower* in 1920. Eugenie Leontovich was to be fatally identified with exotic and mysterious females (*Grand Hotel*, 1930; *Dark Eyes*, 1943; *Anastasia*, 1954).[24] A two-page feature by Helen Ormsbee in the *New York Herald Tribune,* which ran just before the opening (10 February 1935), called attention to the diverse backgrounds and performance traditions of the play's "Three Distinguished Actresses." Thus O'Neil, we are told, "began in a stock company in San Francisco," while Leontovich "came from the Imperial Theater, Moscow"; and while the former "dresses as unaffectedly as she talks," the latter has "the kind of eyes Americans think Russians ought to have." In keeping with her exotic appearance, Leontovich is reported as expressing a gestural, instinctive model of acting:

"To act you must be like this." Here she raised her arms in an expansive upward gesture. "I think every night in the theater a miracle happens. You come into your dressing room, take off your muddy galoshes. . . . Soon, you walk out on the stage, and you are somebody else – somebody quite different from the person who took off the galoshes. That is the miracle."

O'Neil is more pragmatic:

"Two things make acting. . . . One of these things is the player's power to lose himself in the character he plays, and the second is his power to detach a part of his mind at the same time, and use it as a control. This part stands by, watching the other."

Newspaper reports of O'Neil's "booming voice" in *Bodas de sangre* suggest that, like Leontovich, she chose in this case to lose herself in the character; and newspaper portraits of the pair in black mantillas show them striking similar poses. But the process of fusion and

of splitting that O'Neil identifies as acting (of introjecting of the
other and of submitting that identification to a critical agency) is
precisely that which Freud characterizes as obsessive mourning and
melancholia, and to which I will return when I discuss the play itself.

The final mediation between playwright and audience (after
production company, critics, and actors) is the figure of the playwright himself. And already for this first U.S. production, the out-
lines of the Lorca cult clearly emerge. In a lengthy piece, "Lorca
the Andalusian" (*New York Herald Tribune,* 24 February 1935), Mild-
wred Adams claims that "it is impossible to leave Federico García
Lorca out of consideration of his play" and engages in a kind of
fanciful physiognomic study:

A round faced stocky young man, with black brows and hair and warm
brown eyes, he has the coloring and the broad cheek bones of the
gypsy in a mobile, sensitive face, changing with every idea, histrionic
in its quick ability to mirror a mood; a warm, husky voice; a hand
whose short and stubby fingers hardly can stretch an octave.

The "curiously intense civilization" of García Lorca's native Granada has, we are told, "roots . . . deep in the soil." It is vocabulary
still used by modern Spanish editors of *Bodas de sangre,* who contrast
Andalusian telluric tradition with New York deracinated modernity.

Authorialism, "racial" physiognomy, elemental antiquity – such
clichés influenced U.S. audiences then and now. More immediate,
however, is the question of translation. Recent translators have
insisted on the playability of English-language versions of García
Lorca and on the undeniable fact that theater evolves on stage.[25]
The value of the various unpublished versions of Weissberger's texts
is that they show the evolution of what the Neighborhood Playhouse considered a playable version; more particularly, the emendations to the prompt book reproduce the lines as actually spoken
on stage. By contrasting García Lorca's original with Weissberger's
variations and (finally) Hughes's superior version we may glimpse
the ideological assumptions implicit in playability even in a non-
commercial context and reveal those libidinal pressure points at

which the company attempted (unsuccessfully, as it turned out) to protect itself and García Lorca from censure. In this comparative analysis I focus on scenes dealing with mourning, melancholia, and masochism.

3. *"Bitter Oleander," "Fate at the Wedding,"* Mulatto

In the only study of Hughes's translations of which I am aware (one that restricts itself to his versions of Spanish and French verse), one African American scholar cites a model of translation as blood transfusion: "fill[ing] the veins of the poem, nearly emptied through the wound inflicted by the translator, with his own blood."[26] It is a model of introjection and projection to which I will return when I explore the psychic implications of Hughes's version of *Bodas de sangre*. We know that García Lorca himself, who collaborated with José Weissberger, praised the fidelity of the latter's version, calling it "fidelísima." However, fidelity was not simply equivalence: García Lorca explains that "untranslatable" words or phrases were replaced by others suggested by the poet himself to the translator.[27] We may assume that the title was one such inventive substitution. Archival evidence suggests that such trouble in translation focused on poetic diction (florid language), most particularly in relation to the male body.

In Act I, Scene 1, the Mother laments the loss of her dead husband and son:

MADRE: Todo lo que puede cortar el cuerpo de un hombre. Un hombre hermoso, con su flor en la boca, que sale a las viñas o va a sus olivos propios, porque son de él heredados. . . . Y ese hombre no vuelve. O si vuelve es para ponerle una palma encima o un plato de sal gorda para que no se hinche. (I, 1, 4)[28]

Weissberger's version in the prompt book runs as follows:

MOTHER: Anything that can cut into the flesh (body) of a man. A fine [beautiful] man [in the flower of his youth], who goes out WITH A FLOWER IN HIS MOUTH to his own vineyard and to his olive

grove [with a flower in his mouth] because they are his and his
inheritance. . . . And that man doesn't come back. Or if he does,
only to have a palm leaf put upon him or a plate of salt so he should
not swell. (I, 1, 2)[29]

García Lorca's text is an early example of that exclusive devotion to
mourning that Freud called pathological or melancholic. The successive revisions and emendations of the prompt book, however
(much more frequent than elsewhere in the text), betray a nervousness with both García Lorca's lyrical language and its applica-
tion to the aestheticised or eroticized male body, even as it lies rigid
and swollen in death. Exemplary here are the compulsive repetitions of "flower" and the literal bracketing of "body." Note also the
excessive fidelity of the English reproduction of the Spanish sub-
junctive ("so he should not swell"), clumsily archaic. Hughes's
translation, unproduced until 1992, is unerringly physical:

MOTHER: Anything that can split the body of a man apart – a fine
looking man, with a flower in his mouth, starting out to his vine-
yards or his olive trees. His, handed down to him . . . Then that man
doesn't come back. Or if he does come back, it's with a palm on his
breast, or a saucer of rock salt sprinkled on his body to keep it from
swelling. (I, 1, 1–2)[30]

Both lyricism and eroticism emerge unscathed. Hughes's sensitivity
to folk and oral idiom reappears in his versions of García Lorca's
songs. The refrain of the lullaby in Act I, Scene 2 ("Duérmete,
clavel,/que el caballo no quiere beber"), was rightly ridiculed by the
New York critics in Weissberger's clumsy "Sleep, my carnation,/The
horse refuses to drink" (I, 2, [1]). Hughes's version is perfectly simple: "Sleep, little pink/The horse won't drink" (I, 2, 9).

Elsewhere the Neighborhood Playhouse's hostility to male
beauty is combined with prudery. The mother presents her son to
his prospective father-in-law thus: "Mi hijo es hermoso. No ha cono-
cido mujer. La honra más limpia que una sábana puesta al sol" (I,
3, 21). Weissberger: "My son is good. [He does not know women.]
His honor is as bright as linen sheets in the sun" (I, 3, 4). And
Hughes: "My son is handsome. He's never had a woman. He's as

clean as a sheet in the sun" (I, 3, 3). Compare the servant's forth-right praise of marriage to the bride. García Lorca: "¡Dichosa tú que vas a abrazar a un hombre, que lo vas a besar, que vas a sentir su peso!" (II, 1, p. 27). Weissberger: "Happy you who will embrace a man! How you will kiss him" (II, 1, [1]). And Hughes: "Happy girl, about to hold a man in your arms, to kiss him, to feel his weight on your body" (II, 1, 22). While Weissberger flees from physicality, Hughes inserts the word "body," absent in the original, further to bring out the erotic reference of the text.

The mother's marital advice to her son in the same act receives similar treatment:

MADRE: Con tu mujer procura estar cariñoso, y si la notas infatuada o arisca, hazle una caricia que le produzca un poco de daño, un abrazo fuerte, un mordisco y luego un beso suave. Que ella no pueda disgustarse, pero que sienta que tú eres el macho, el amo, el que mandas. (II, 2, 49)

MOTHER: with your wife, try to be always tender and if you find her wayward or reserved, caress her [but so that it hurts her a bit; a strong embrace, a bite and then a soft kiss, in a way that cannot make her angry;] but so that she feels you are the master, the one that commands. (Weissberger, II, 2, 13)

MOTHER: Try to be always loving with your wife. And if sometimes she's touchy and mean, pet her in a way that hurts her a little, a big hug, a bite – and then a gentle kiss after that. Not enough to make her angry, but enough to let her know you're a man, and the one that runs things. (Hughes, II, 2, 9)

The slight suggestion of sadism here clearly proved unsettling to a Broadway audience, even one schooled in the progressive ethno-graphic and aesthetic innovations of "little theater." Yet more trou-bling is the extravagant masochism of the bride in the final act after the elopement with Leonardo:

NOVIA: ... Con los dientes,
              con las manos, como puedas,
              quita de mi cuello honrado
              el metal de esta cadena,

dejándome arrinconada
allá en mi casa de tierra.
Y si no quieres matarme
como a víbora pequeña,
pon en mis manos de novia
el cañón de la escopeta.

. . .

Y yo dormiré a tus pies
para guardar lo que sueñas.
Desnuda, mirando al campo,

(*Dramática*)

como si fuera una perra,
¡porque eso soy! Que te miro
y tu hermosura me quema.
     (García Lorca, III, 1, 60, 62)

NOVIA: With your hands, with your teeth,
However you can, strike off my chains.
Or if you will not, kill me
As one kills a small adder.
[Give me in my own two hands
The barrel of the gun.]
. . .
I will sleep at your feet
To behold what you dream.

(*Dramatically*)

As if I were a watchdog,
For that's what I am.
I am gazing upon you
And I am burned by the flame of your being.
     (Weissberger, III, 1, 4, 6)

GIRL: Take your teeth, take your hands, take whatever you can and
break the chain of purity about my neck, and throw me in a corner

there in a cave. And if you don't kill me like a little serpent, then give me the mouth of your gun in my hands. . . . I'll sleep at your feet, watching over your dreams. Naked at your feet, like a dog. When I look at you, your beauty burns me, consumes me. (Hughes, III, 1, 7, 8)

The passage exhibits that passionate self-denigration that for Freud is characteristic of both melancholia and masochism. While Weissberger attempts to reproduce García Lorca's poetic form, he distances the erotic scene with archaic diction ("behold") and fussily precise grammar ("as if I were a watchdog"). Hughes, on the other hand, abandons the verse form but heightens the rhythmic pleasure of García Lorca's amorous desolation through affective vocabulary and urgent, idiomatic syntax ("Naked at your feet, like a dog"). Note also Hughes's anthropomorphic "mouth of the gun" (as opposed to Weissberger's "barrel of the gun," itself edited out in performance), the source of a fatally amorous introjection or incorporation.

We come now to the last scene of the play, in which the Mother and Bride lament the mutual penetration of the two male rivals:

MADRE: . . . se mataron los dos hombres del amor.
   Con un cuchillo,
   con un cuchillito,
   que apenas cabe en la mano,
   pero que penetra fino
   por las carnes asombradas,
   y que se para en el sitio
   donde tiemble enmarañada
   la oscura raíz del grito.
       (García Lorca, III, 2, 72)

MOTHER: Two men killed one another for love.
   With a knife
   With a little knife
   That hardly fills the hand.
   But that penetrates [sharply] finely
   The astonished flesh.

And stops on the spot
Where trembles deeply embedded
The dark root of a scream.
                    (Weissberger, III, 2, 7)

MOTHER: . . . two men in love killed each other. With a knife, with a
   little knife almost too small to hold in your hand, but sharp enough
   to find its way through tangled flesh, to stop entangled in the trembling roots of a cry. (Hughes, III, 2, 7)

We have seen that Hughes's language (unlike Weissberger's) is
poetic, but not pretentious, and plain, but not banal; and that
(again unlike Weissberger) he scrupulously avoids all falsely exotic
or particularizing detail (note that Hughes's partners are simply
"boy" and "girl," as opposed to Weissberger's "novio" and "novia").
In this final quotation, however, we find most explicitly that eroticization of the male body which is shared by García Lorca and
Hughes. This is a body that is (in Hughes's words), swollen, hard,
and rigid; but that tumescence is bought only at the price of death
and more particularly the incorporation of the other man's deadly
beauty – the small, pointed instrument that finds it way to the tangled root of a man in love. I argue later that the male body as lost
object is at the center of García Lorca's practice of tragedy. But
in his hints of anal intercourse here (as in his previous uncom-
promising versions of mourning, melancholia, and masochism),
Hughes not only outdoes the timid and precious formalism of
Weissberger and the Neighborhood Playhouse; he also reenacts
that dissolution or surrender of the African American translator to
the Spanish poet, that radical blood transfusion, in which the subject takes on the introjected qualities of the other even as it
destroys him and splits his body apart.

On the back of Brooks Atkinson's review of *Bodas de sangre* the *New
York Times* carried an anonymous report titled: "Protests bar show
of art on lynching/Macabre exhibition canceled on 'outburst' of
objections from secret sources." García Lorca's version of the
blood feud, which ends with a deadly posse, was thus simultaneous

in 1935 with artistic attempts to raise the incendiary question of racist violence. Hughes's *Mulatto,* staged at the Vanderbilt Theater on 24 October 1935, was another attempt to address the same "social message" as the anonymous art curators, and one whose climax is a lynch party cheated of its prey by suicide.[31] Unlike *Bodas de sangre, Mulatto* was to be a commercial success, the longest-running play on Broadway by an African American author to that date.[32] And unlike García Lorca, whose play was adapted and staged by sympathetic collaborators, Hughes was the victim of distortion and extortion in the production of his "Tragedy of the Deep South" – the text was mutilated and the royalties were appropriated by the white producer.[33]

Like those of its fellow unlikely participant in the 1935 season, however, *Mulatto*'s poor notices focused on poetic diction: Arthur Pollock in the *Brooklyn Daily Eagle* of 25 October lamented the lack of the "flavor of rich Negro speech" white audiences required of a "race" play. As with *Bodas de sangre* once more, Brooks Atkinson in the *New York Times* of the same date gives the most sympathetic appraisal, praising Hughes for his "sincerity" in addressing the subjection of his race but lamenting the play's "fatal weakness as drama." But just as Nance O'Neil's dignified Mother salvaged the tragic tone of *Bodas de sangre,* so distinguished veteran Rose McClendon as Hughes's mourning matriarch transcended the text. As Atkinson wrote: "It is always a privilege to see her adding fineness of perception to the parts she takes." It was to prove the last part taken by this "gallant artist."[34]

If *Bodas de sangre* stages the merger of feuding lovers and dueling men, *Mulatto* dramatizes the pleasure and the danger of racial fusion – the light-skinned "yellow" son of a white colonel and his black mistress demands entrance into white society. And if *Bodas de sangre* has no equivalent of *Mulatto*'s castrating father,[35] both plays culminate in the lament of mourning mothers for sacrificed sons. *Mulatto* opens with expository dialogue and description – the scene is the Big House on a plantation in Georgia, where Colonel Thomas lives (exceptionally) with his long-time black mistress, Cora.[36] Their light-skinned teenage children, Bert and Sallie, are currently visiting from the North, where they have been sent to be educated. If the detail here is fussy and naturalistic compared with that in García Lorca, still critics note that Hughes gives fewer folksy southern regionalisms than his Broadway predecessors.[37] Moreover, references to previous lynchings set up an ominous tragic back story analogous to García Lorca's blood feud, which is likewise already in place when the action begins.

As in *Bodas de sangre,* the drama is motivated by filiation – the supposed trace of blood from father to son; and as in *Bodas de sangre* once more it is the mother who is granted the prediction motif: "I's scared to death for de boy. . . . [T]hese white folks'll kill him" (I, 14). In the mother's proleptic mourning, naturalism cedes, as in García Lorca, to vibrant lyricism and stylized lament:

CORA: Oh, Lawd, have mercy! (Beginning to cry) I don't know what to do. De way he's acting up can't go on. . . . Somethin's gonna happen to ma chile. I had a bad dream last night, too, and I looked out and seed de moon all red with blood. I seed a path o' living blood across this house, I tell you, in my sleep. Oh, Lawd, have mercy! (Sobbing) Oh, Lawd, help me in ma troubles. (I, 15)

The Lorcan iconography, anticipated by Hughes, is transparent. More important perhaps is the engagement with popular vernacular and idiom also shared with García Lorca, the appeal to oral rhythm, and visual imagery for dramatic intensification. Note also the projection and introjection of the blood – drawn out from the son and into the moon and house.

The mother's tears and sobs testify to her melancholy; and when in Act II her son kills the father who will not recognize him, mourning becomes madness: Cora, in Freud's words "turn[s] away from reality . . . cling[s] to the object through . . . hallucinatory wishful psychosis" (p. 253). In the first of two great monologues, Cora pleads with the dead colonel to protect their son, now pursued by the lynch mob. The mother's masochistic self-recrimination ("I been sleeping with you too long") is enhanced by dramatic lighting effects: "In the sky the twilight deepens into early night. CORA stands looking into the darkness" (II, 1, 26– 7).

Mulatto thus problematizes the question of dramatic diction. Robert, the educated mulatto, is told by his father to "talk right . . . like a nigger" (II, 1, 24). And as the tragic action develops, Hughes elaborates a lyrical language based intermittently on folk idiom and supplemented by affective stage directions. Thus the mother's monologues are juxtaposed with the figure of the righteously homicidal and sacrificial son: "ROBERT drops the body of his father at [Cora's] feet in a path of flame from the setting sun" (II, 1, 24); or again: "He exits slowly, tall and straight against the sun" (II, 1, 25). *Mulatto's* progressive elevation of diction, abstraction of reference, and intensification of tragic action thus come to focus (as in *Bodas de sangre*) on the lost body of a proud and attractive young man, described here in the cast list as "Eighteen . . .; strong and well-built; a light mulatto with ivory-yellow skin and proud thin features . . . of a fiery, impetuous temper . . . resenting his blood and the circumstances of his birth" (p. 2). Given, like García Lorca's Leonardo, to racing across the country (here in his father's Ford, not on a horse), Bert is the lost love object on whose inevitable annihilation the plot is wholly dependent.

If *Mulatto* is quite clearly a drama of social assimilation (the mulatto demands entrance into white society) and familial identification (he demands recognition from his father), it is also, and less evidently, a tragedy of incorporation or, more properly, introjection in which fantasies of bodily borders map onto the scenic space: Hughes thus dramatizes that "function of judgment" which for Freud is based on the most archaic of libidinal preferences: "I should like to take this into myself or keep it out."[38] The intolerability of miscegenation was held to lie in its breaching of all-too-permeable boundaries. Likewise the focus of Hughes's drama is a series of transgressive entrances into the Big House: Robert's crime is repeatedly to penetrate the front door from which he is forbidden by birth to enter. The fear of and fascination with fusion (with "mixtries"), with the absorption of the qualities of the introjected object, are thus rendered immediately dramatic by Hughes in the stage movements of his central character. But if the object will be violently rejected or kept out by the hostile social body, still that negation cannot prevent a measure of redemption: In the final scene Robert returns to the House by the front door, choosing suicide by his own hand, rather than lynching by others; and Cora, grieving and brutalized, confronts the raging mob with calm resolution. Hughes writes: "It is as though no human hand can touch her again" (II, 2, 35).

While García Lorca's plot proved familiar to Broadway audiences, Hughes's was so novel as to be incendiary, truly testing the limits of New York commercial theater in the period. As an intertext for *Bodas de sangre*, however, and as its contemporary in the generally mediocre 1935 season, *Mulatto* offers three insights into *Bodas de sangre*. The first is that lyrical language is not incompatible with urgent social concerns – Hughes's bloody moons and heavily symbolic sunsets do not detract from but rather heighten his political message. The second is that familial or domestic drama need not be isolated from the broadest of historical issues – in this case the intolerable legacy of slavery and segregation. The third is that the trappings of tragedy (of heredity, determinism, and the prediction motif) can be invoked without implying that the outcome is inevitable – still the subject retains a measure of freedom of choice and will. Hughes thus uses the symbolics of blood to challenge and not to confirm the racism with which that image repertoire is, nonetheless, associated. The challenge posed by *Mulatto* to *Bodas de sangre*, then, is the same as that posed by Hughes's translation of García Lorca's play – it is the challenge of introjection (of absorption and of negation), of incorporating an other that tends (pleasurably, dangerously, dramatically) to split the self.

4. Mourning, Melancholia, Masochism

The tragic mechanism of *Bodas de sangre* is motivated by the fear of mixed blood. As the posse pursues the fugitive lovers, one woodcutter predicts that by the time they are caught their blood will have mixed ("mezclado"). Another replies that such is the destiny of the groom's "caste," a caste of men who lie dead in the street ("su casta de muertos en mitad de la calle"; III, 1, 53). By the end of the play the fugitive heterosexual couple will have been replaced by a homosexual pair, rigid and bloodless – Hughes's "two men in love." Recent critics have called attention to the play's elements of homo-eroticism or gender merger. Thus for one *Bodas de sangre* marks a "turning away from the site of procreative intercourse" toward "more shameful proclivities," a "therapeutic release" that serves as an "oblique apologia for [García Lorca's] permanent bachelor-hood."[39] Another rehearses the repeated examples of inverted gender roles in the play, claiming that women triumph over the bodies of the men whom they have led to death.[40] It is clear from such cases that psychoanalytically informed readings can be simply homo-phobic and misogynistic. By rereading the play in the light of some texts by Freud, I aim, however, to raise once more the questions of homosexual desire and authorial agency, but in a new, more sym-pathetic light.

It would be easy to compile case studies of García Lorca's char-acters in the light of Freud's theories of mourning, melancholia, and masochism. Hence, the Mother, willingly confined to her house, appears to exhibit the symptoms of pathological mourning: "dejection, cessation of interest in the outside world . . . inhibition of activity" (p. 252); or again she insists on bringing up "each sin-gle one of the memories . . . in which the libido is bound" (p. 253). As she turns away from reality, the persistence of her mourning bears out Freud's dry observation that "people never willingly abandon a libidinal position" (p. 253).

The bride, on the other hand, appears to exhibit melancholia – fruit, Freud says, of "real or imagined object-loss" (p. 254): "the patient . . . reproaches himself, vilifies himself, and expects to be cast out and punished [in] . . . an overcoming of the instinct which compels every living thing to cling to life" (p. 254). As Freud remarks once more: "The loss of the love-object is an excellent opportunity for the ambivalence in love-relationships . . . to come into the open" (p. 260). Self-recrimination and reproach, mingled feelings of love and hate – these are characteristic of the bride's dialogue and action before and after she is confronted once more with Leonardo, her lost lover.

However, it would seem vain to offer personalized, psychologi-cal readings of characters who within the play itself are denoted only according to their familial function: Mother, Bride, Groom. And, more particularly, the bride does not share Freud's third pre-condition of melancholia – after loss of the object and ambivalence toward that object comes "regression of the libido into the ego" (p. 267). While the bride is clearly aware of the source of her distress, the "painful wound" of Freud's melancholia derives from an object-loss that is withdrawn from consciousness, substituting a conflict within the ego for the struggle over the object (p. 268). When the object relationship has shattered, in Freud's lyrical phrase: "the shadow of the object fell upon the ego," producing "a cleavage between the critical activity of the ego and the ego as altered by identification [with the loved person]." This splitting is motivated by introjection: "The ego wants to incorporate the object into itself . . . by devouring it" (p. 258).

This sadistic and desiring orality is distributed throughout *Bodas de sangre* and cannot be confined to any single character. Thus the very name of the hated caste fills the mother's mouth with a foul taste that she must spit out ("tengo que escupir"; I, 1, 10); the horse of the lullaby refuses to drink from the river to which it is led ("el caballo no quiere beber"; I, 2, 12); Leonardo tells the bride that he will not be spat out, the way silver spits ("la plata . . . escupe"; II, 1, 30); the wife recalls her wedding day when "the whole countryside fitted in [her] mouth" ("me cabía todo el campo en mi boca"; II, 1, 39); the mother drinks in the blood of her slain son ("Me mojé las manos de sangre y me las lamí con la lengua"; II, 2, 42); and finally the groom, at his moment of fatal destiny, feels the teeth of his family in his flesh ("siento los dientes de todos los míos clavados aquí"; III, 1, 57). While this devouring orality is indeed, as critics have claimed, associated with castration fears (from the unfortunate Rafael, whose arms are torn off by "the machine" ["la máquina"; I, 1, 8] to the exhausted horse of the lullaby, its eyes pierced by a silver dagger ["un puñal de plata"; I, 2, 17]), and archaic orality coincides with gender fusion or inversion (from the groom who is praised for his chastity to the bride able to "cut a rope with her teeth" ["cortar una maroma con los dientes"; I, 3, 21]), these are insufficient to account for the dark cloud that falls over the play as a whole.

I will suggest in a moment that the tragic destiny of García Lorca's "castes" can be at once historicized and libidinalized. The hypothesis I raise now is that there is indeed a missing object (or more properly a missing relation) that is withdrawn from consciousness, the third term proper to pathological mourning and melancholia, one that cannot be allowed to appear on stage and yet enacts the climax of the drama – the object is the male body and the relation is that between desiring male bodies ("two men in love"), who can be represented only in the voices of mourning women and as twin violins, whose sound is cut short by dark cries. Freud speaks of "a love which cannot be given up although the object itself is given up" (p. 260). The all-pervasive melancholia of *Bodas de sangre*, like Hughes's self-effacing translation, testifies, mutely, to just such a love.

That love is also present in the play's masochism. Freud distinguishes between three related forms of masochism: erotogenic ("a condition imposed on sexual excitation"), feminine ("an expression of the feminine nature"), and moral ("a norm of behavior," p. 415). Restricting himself, curiously perhaps, to feminine masochism in men, Freud claims that it "place[s] the subject in a characteristically female situation . . . castrated, copulated with . . . blinded" (pp. 416–17). Erotogenic masochism can be primary ("libidinally bound sadism . . . remains inside [the subject]") or secondary ("projected [and] once more introjected [by the subject]") (pp. 418–19). It may appear as oral ("the fear of being eaten up"); as sadistic-anal ("the wish to be beaten"); or phallic ("castration") (p. 419). We have already noted examples of such masochism in *Bodas de sangre*, most spectacularly in the scene where the bride compares herself to a snake or dog and asks for the "mouth" of Leonardo's gun. Hence although orality is the prototype of incorporation, the latter expands to include other bodily functions ("the skin, respiration, sight, hearing"),[41] a process facilitated by introjection that "does not necessarily imply any reference to the body's real boundaries."[42] One example of this extended eroticization of bodily functions is the bride's amorous submission to Leonardo at her wedding – trembling, she claims that she cannot hear his voice; that she feels as if she had drunk a whole bottle of *anís* and had gone to sleep on a coverlet of roses; and that she is being dragged along and suffocated in spite of herself (II, 1, 32). All five senses are incorporated here.[43] Elsewhere the body's boundaries are mapped onto the scenic space (as in Hughes's *Mulatto*) – the bride is initially enclosed by the round cave with its circular windows (I, 3, 18), from which she makes a ceremonial exit to go to the wedding (II, 1, 37). Finally, she will stand at the doorway of her mother-in-law's house, forbidden to enter (III, 2, 71). During the posse sequence, the moon demands entrance to both roof tiles and breasts (houses and bodies) (III, 1, 55). The twin circles of the festive round dance at the wedding and the fatal "circle of men" in the forest reenact the same twinning of the social and the physical to equally dramatic effect.

This generalization and depersonalization of masochism (as of melancholia) in *Bodas de sangre* suggest an economy of pleasure and unpleasure such as that sketched by Freud at the start of his essay:

> Pleasure and unpleasure . . . cannot be referred to an increase or decrease of a quantity (which we describe as "tension due to stimulus") . . . but on some qualitative characteristic. . . . Perhaps it is the *rhythm*, the temporal sequence of changes, rises and falls in the quantity of stimulus. (p. 414)

An economic model of drama would transcend character and author. And it would account for both the rhythmic quality of García Lorca's theater (as in the criss-crossing of the stage by actors in Act II) and for the curious lessening of tension in Act III (as in the slower soliloquies of Moon and Death). For, as Freud remarks, tension can sometimes be pleasurable, just as the lessening of tension can be unpleasurable. In other words, we must pay as much attention to the quality (kind) as to the quantity (amount) of stimulus. If, as the mother claims, "Everyone likes to find out what ails them" ("A cada uno le gusta enterarse de lo que le duele" [I, 1, 10]), then that pleasurable displeasure is communicated and experienced economically – through a rhythmic, temporal sequence of reserve and release. The Neighborhood Playhouse's preference for music and movement over text might well correspond to such an economy.

Freud's final form of masochism is moral, that which he describes as a "norm of behavior" (p. 415). Here masochism has "loosened its connection with what we recognize as sexuality" (p. 429). Moral masochism is associated with an "unconscious sense of guilt" or more properly a "need for punishment" from the introjected parents:

The last figure in the series that began with the parents is the dark power of Destiny which only the fewest of us are able to look upon as impersonal. . . . In order to provoke punishment from this last representative of the parents, the masochist must . . . ruin the prospects which open up to him in the real world and must, perhaps, destroy his own real existence. (pp. 423, 425)

For Freud, then, that archaic choice of eating or spitting out thus leads finally (in the inevitable introjection of the parents) to the emergence of a function of judgment and a sense of fatality. Moral masochism seems to explain the bride's persistent and perverse pride in her continued virginity after the bloody death of the male rivals. Just as love outlives its object, so the need for punishment from the parental figure (society, the mother-in-law) outstrips the perceived fault committed – as Freud notes, "the true masochist always turns his cheek whenever he has a chance of receiving a blow" (p. 420). But much more broadly, moral masochism suggests a new reading of the fatality so ubiquitous and so hackneyed in *Bodas de sangre* and the figure of García Lorca in general. For that Destiny which even Freud can barely see as impersonal, which compels the subject to destroy his own real existence, is by no means inevitable but is rather the result of a "cultural suppression of the instincts" (p. 425). The introjection of parental authority (as when the groom feels his family sink their teeth into his back) is not, then, simply personal or psychic; rather, as García Lorca quite clearly demonstrates, it is the result of specific social conventions – the exchange of women and the prohibition of relations between

men. If, then, as Freud claims, we are "linked to Destiny by libidinal ties" and that "through moral masochism, morality becomes
sexualized once more" (pp. 423, 424), this is no blind bodily urge
seeking extinction. Rather, this is eros as tamer of the death wish,
with García Lorca as master of a libidinal economy, whose losses
are finally, pleasurably, made good.

5. Prophetic Tragedy

Langston Hughes's translation of *Bodas de sangre* was not staged
until the New York Public Theater's production of 1992. The
resulting mixed notices recalled the Neighborhood Playhouse's
version almost sixty years earlier. The *New York Times* praised the
"lyrical" translation but lamented that its "heightened language"
led African American veteran Gloria Foster as the mother to an
overdramatic performance style.[44] *New York* magazine was frankly
hostile, attacking the hybridity of both cast and production style
and branding Foster "hysterical."[45] The *Village Voice* wrote rather of
the "mixed blessings of multiculturalism": The actors' varied
accents and backgrounds, the mélange of incidental music (*cante
jondo* and jazz) and scenic design (naturalistic and abstract) – all
these elements rendered García Lorca's unified conception of
"fate" obsolete in the context of contemporary fragmented reality.[46] Although it found Foster excessively mannered ("Gloria in
extremis"), the *Voice* did, however, note the connection between
Bodas de sangre's "somber outlook" and the "sorrow" of African
Americans. Language, reference, and genre were thus updated by
critics for a newly diverse New York theater.

This chapter has been in part an homage to the fragile legacy of
three distinguished actresses in the roles of García Lorca's and
Hughes's mourning mothers: Nance O'Neil, Rose McClendon,
and Gloria Foster. I suggest, however, that in its focus on fatality,
García Lorca's tragedy may not be as unified as contemporary
reviewers might suppose. One contemporary scholar who has elaborated a powerful account of hybridity, prophecy, and tragedy in
response to the current condition of African Americans is Cornel

West. Drawing on traditions as diverse as Marxism, pragmatism, and black spirituality, West proposes the tragic as a sense of the absolute "irrevocability of deeds."[47] Avoiding both the social determinism of the left (which denies citizens responsibility for their actions) and the abstract idealism of the right (which denies the dehumanizing effect of social structures),[48] West argues for a sense of ethical responsibility toward the future (a sense of prophecy) that he sees as characteristically North American, based as it is on voluntarism, fallibilism, and experimentalism.[49]

This twin sense of an irrevocable past (disabused pessimism) and a possible future (qualified and strenuous optimism) might inspire a rereading of *Bodas de sangre* and García Lorca, weighted down as both are by deterministic notions of fatality that deny the will and the freedom of both characters and author. Such a stress on the future appears, however, to be incompatible with psychoanalysis's interrogation of the past (of the subject, of society). Yet I have argued that the Freudian process of introjection that is characteristic of both theatrical performance and translation involves the modulation or transformation of the subject in its perilous merger with the other – a rhythmic disposition of movement in time analogous to the libidinal economy of mourning, melancholia, and masochism. Langston Hughes's translation, performed only after his death, is a fine example of that risky and unpredictable promise of the future that is characteristic of both cultural hybridity and psychic fusion. For West, as for Hughes, African American musics such as blues and jazz are another.[50] Freud himself attacks as "hysterical symptoms" the architectural monuments to a great city's painful history, reminiscent of the psychic life of those hysterics and neurotics who "cannot get free from the past and for its sake . . . neglect what is real and immediate."[51] We risk identifying with Freud's "impractical Londoners," grieving before the tomb of a medieval queen, if we cling too reverently to such cultural monuments as García Lorca, failing to allow for fallibility and experiment in the development and interpretation of their work.

This is particularly true of drama, which exists primarily in performance (Freud's "temporal sequence of changes . . . in the quantity of stimulus"). Thus if I have argued for a distinctively North American or African American reading of García Lorca (in Broadway critics and in "little theater" productions, in twin, contradictory translations), then that reading reaches out, inevitably, to others, most particularly to those Spaniards who argue, erroneously, that New York has no history and in whose own country the performance tradition of García Lorca was disrupted for so long by the Dictatorship. Moreover, if Spanish critics and producers of *Bodas de sangre* have tended to place undue emphasis on "a sense of land" (on an elemental Andalusia contrasted with a deracinated North America),[52] then they have also tended to repress those aspects of García Lorca's achievement that fail to reconfirm such stereotypes. Just as it was an African American translator who discreetly reasserted the homoeroticism of *Bodas de sangre* in the 1930s, so in recent years it has been U.S. critics who have drawn attention to García Lorca's repeated affirmation during the years in which he wrote the so-called rural trilogy that the earlier and projected plays on homosexuality (*El público, Las hijas de Lot*) constituted his real, true theater.[53] If the desirable male body is the lost object of *Bodas de sangre,* exiled off stage, so García Lorca's "unrepresentable" or "unplayable" plays are the absent center of his dramatic career, that risky future possibility which critics' cult of the past seeks to obscure. "Black wedding" (the title of this chapter) thus refers not only to the bride's black dress, whether it is taken as traditional costume or a symbol of mourning,[54] nor to Hughes's vibrant African American reading, unproduced for so long; rather, it points the way to a future ethical reading of García Lorca's drama as the once unrepresentable relation to the male body, a relation that is both a risky, experimental possibility and an irrevocable deed, mourned and remembered as the spectacle of dark love.

3

Poet in Paris

Así que pasen cinco años (*When Five Years Have Passed*),
Corydon, and the Truth of Anamnesis

1. The Truth of the Life

Así que pasen cinco años is the most enigmatic and problematic of
García Lorca's plays.[1] An outline of the plot is as follows: A Young
Man hopes to marry his fifteen-year-old Fiancée on her return from
a journey of five years' duration. When the period has elapsed, he
seeks her out, but she rejects him and runs off with a Rugby Player.
Remembering the existence of the Typist whose advances he had
previously rejected, he goes in search of this second woman. When
she insists herself on a five-year postponement of their love, the
Young Man returns home and dies when he plays "hearts" at a fatal
card game. This central action is repeatedly interrupted by secondary figures of a decidedly non-naturalistic character: a Dead Cat
and Child; a Mannequin, longing for marriage; a Girl, whose lover
has drowned; a sinister Clown and Harlequin; and a Yellow Mask,
also mourning a lost lover and child.

In spite of the extreme difficulty of the text, there is at first sight
a curious critical unanimity concerning its significance. The multiple male characters of Act I (Old Man and First and Second
Friends) are read as alter egos of the main character (the Young
Man) and as representatives of three relations to time – future, present, and past, respectively.[2] Likewise the external locations of the
three Acts (the Young Man's library, his Fiancée's bedroom, and a
mysterious forest containing a miniature theater) are reduced to
one.[3] This is taken to be that interior space in which the Young Man
plays out or works through his psychic traumas or phobias – the
rejection of marriage, the missed encounter with the woman, the
sterility of children who will never be born. Whether the antecedents of the play are taken to be surrealist or (as they have been

71

more recently) expressionist,[4] there is a consensus that the temporal, spatial, and subjective fragments of *Así que pasen cinco años* may be traced back to a single, solitary figure, frequently identified with the playwright himself. Moreover, it is now generally accepted that the lyrically oneiric atmosphere of the play is derived from García Lorca's knowledge of Freud's *Interpretation of Dreams*.[5] That familiarity is thought to make itself manifest either in a literalist vein (the action of the play is simply the dream of the character within it) or in a more subtle, structural mode (the composition of the play exhibits patterns characteristic of the dream-work).[6]

I will suggest in this chapter, however, both that the play should not be reduced to a monologue or disguised autobiography and that the psychologist criticism that does so is sustained by a hidden but productive contradiction – that between anecdote and allegory. I take anecdote to be reference without resonance, and, inversely, allegory to be resonance without reference. As pure denotation, anecdote invokes a singular, historical plane that resists interpretation. For example, Margarita Ucelay, the author of a recent critical edition of *Así que pasen cinco años*, is only the most recent critic to cite Frederico's sister Isabel as witness to the supposedly descriptive nature of the text. Episodes such as the stoning to death of the Cat, disguises such as the Harlequin and Clown costumes, locations such as the theater within the theater (whose prototype is held to be a stairwell in the family home), and actions such as the repetition of clock chimes – each of these elements of the play is said to be derived directly from childhood memory (Ucelay, p. 143). Inversely, however, the "autobiographical image" can be "inverted" (p. 62) or subjected to a chain of allegorical associations – a reference to "anemone" suggests to Ucelay "narcissus" and hence the sterile fate of the Young Man (of García Lorca), who dies without realizing his true self (pp. 88–9). Here poetic resonance or connotation is all, and the historical fact of childlessness yields to the imagistic lyricism of the sterile flower, an allegory of hysteria and perhaps of homosexuality to which, incidentally, Freud's early collaborator Breuer also refers.[7]

The personal prestige of testimony is, however, undermined by the fallibility of memory: Ucelay writes elsewhere that Isabel García Lorca "*vaguely* remembers *some* clown or harlequin costume which lay forgotten in trunks *or* old wardrobes" (my emphasis, p. 52). And anecdote and allegory are collapsed in two crucial areas – the prediction motif as truth of the death and homosexuality as truth of the life.[8] It seems that no critic can resist citing the coincidence that García Lorca was killed almost exactly five years after he finished writing *Así que pasen cinco años*. Even Francisco García Lorca, who writes that in the case of the Yellow Mask "the great merit of the dramatist . . . lies in the fact that he does not give us the biography of the character," does not shrink from mentioning "the disturbing, premonitory resonance" of the time period.[9] We shall see that for Freud no period of time can be indifferent in psychoanalysis; and for Lorca critics, this strictly anecdotal detail (Ucelay cites a favorite childhood reading of Victor Hugo as a possible source)[10] is endowed with the transcendent value of mortality. Likewise, the status of the Young Man's frustration, narcissism, abulia, and sterility is undecided – on the one hand it is thought to correspond to the biographical condition of García Lorca, who, like the Mannequin in the play, has lost the wedding ring (II, p. 281); on the other, it is held to be emblematic of the existential anguish of author and character's human essence, the key to the truth of the life.[11] The emergence of homosexuality as a theme in García Lorca criticism is thus split between anecdote and allegory – between an urge to acknowledge the experience of the historical García Lorca and a desire to impose a transcendent meaning on a text (*Así que pasen cinco años*) that, unlike *El público*, does not speak aloud that meaning, reticently refuses to confess the truth of the self.[12]

That truth first emerged in France and is one of the reasons why a French Lorca (like a French Freud) is particularly distinctive and deserves separate study. In this chapter I will address the performance history of García Lorca in France, concentrating on a polemical production of *Así que pasen cinco años* in translation by the noted Lorca biographer Marcelle Auclair. I go on to contrast the

pseudonymous Jean-Louis Schonberg's scandalous studies of García Lorca[13] with those of Auclair herself, exemplarily reticent and
hesitant, even as she appeals to personal testimony as García
Lorca's friend.[14] Schonberg's obsessive and lurid reiteration of
García Lorca's "Corydonianism" (the most transparent of projected fantasies) leads me to Gide's dialogue *Corydon*, published in
Spanish translation with an "anti-Socratic" prologue by Gregorio
Marañón.[15] More desired than desiring, prone to hesitation and
delay, the Gidian youth casts an unexpected light on García
Lorca's Young Man; and Gide's theory of a masculine identified
pederasty underwritten by natural law and human history enables
us to reread relations between men in *Así que pasen cinco años*, relations that have generally been collapsed into solitary narcissism.

Finally I invoke the case history in Freud. Anamnesis, the patient's retelling of his or her own story, is etymologically derived
from memory. Remembering (and thus inventing psychoanalysis),
early patients such as Dora revealed the inextricable interaction of
memory and fantasy in a life history.[16] Moreover, the fragmented
nature of that history is for Freud not simply anecdotal but rather
theoretically functional in the parallel but separate narratives of
neurosis and treatment. Finally, Dora's anamnesis reveals a fluidity
of projection that includes cross-gender identification for both
herself and for Freud – her deepest love (and the one that repeatedly reduces Freud to paralyzed indecision) is for the "adorable
white body" of her father's female lover, Frau K.[17] Placing herself
in her father's place (and placing Freud in hers), Dora points to
the possibility of articulating a repressed homosexuality without
prurience, of fusing the singular, anecdotal event, preserved in
memory, and the general, allegorical meaning, transformed by
fantasy.

The "private theater" of hysteria[18] might be related to the dimin-
utive theater set up on stage in Act III, Scene 1, of *Así que pasen cinco
años*. Certainly, both are related in complex but undeniable ways to
the public performances of the social and historical world (the
miniature theater has a staircase leading from it to the stage proper
below). And for Freud, as for García Lorca and his critics, anecdote

and death are mutually constitutive – the punning slip of Freud's collaborator Sandor Ferenczi, *Anectode*,[19] prefigures the death wish of García Lorca's biographers, which persists even as they strive obsessively to elucidate ever more minute details of the life. Moreover, as we shall see, each of our narratives (that of García Lorca, of Gide, and of Freud) is based on a rejected proposal and a postponed engagement. Far from being deadly as critics have invariably proposed, this deferral for a fixed period is productive of desire – of theater, of sexuality, and of interpretation.

2. Paris 1958; Schonberg and Auclair

In her exhaustive study of cross-cultural contacts between Spanish and French theater, Phyllis Zatlin notes that García Lorca is one of only two Spanish dramatists who could claim to be fully "integrated" into the postwar French stage.[20] Indeed, most unusually for a Spanish dramatist, productions of García Lorca in France in the period were much more frequent in French than in Spanish, in spite of the large exile community to which original-language productions were dedicated (p. 19). García Lorca's popularity in Paris for two decades after 1945 gave rise to what has been called a "Lorca myth in France" (p. 49). Productions peaked in the early 1960s; four ran simultaneously in Paris in the season of 1963–4 (p. 50). Famous productions preceding the premiere of *Así que pasen cinco años* included *Bernarda Alba* (1945–6), *Yerma* (1954), and *Don Perlimplín* (1957). Zatlin cites "two opposing tendencies" in French productions – stylized abstraction and folkloric *espagnolade* (p. 54). It seems that French audiences were more accustomed to the latter than the former, that abstraction to which the willfully deracinated text of *Así que pasen cinco años* so clearly lends itself.

Paris Journal announced on 1 December 1958 that "a fifty fifth theater [was] to open in Paris with a previously unstaged Lorca" – it was to be called the Théâtre Récamier. The Ligue Française de l'Enseignement had been responsible for turning this former cinema into a theater and was proposing a programming policy that would not be too avant-garde but would nonetheless favor modern playwrights and young, talented directors. One of these was Guy Suarès, who had directed the prize-winning *Yerma* of 1954. In keeping with its educational ethos, the Récamier would provide children's theater on Thursday matinees, to be followed by discussions on the classics, beginning with *Bérénice*. An Ionesco play was to follow the García Lorca premiere, of which thirty performances were planned. As *Le Parisien Libéré* reconfirmed (4 December 1958), the Récamier seemed "to want to situate itself fair and square under the banner of quality."

In *Les Lettres Françaises* of the same date, Marcelle Auclair, the translator and adapter of the play, noted that "there is no trace in the play of the Spain which Federico so celebrated [elsewhere]"; and confessed her "anxiety" as to the play's reception by the public. The premonition was justified: *L'Intransigeant* reported on 10 December that rehearsals had been suspended, reportedly because of disagreements between the adapter and the director, and on 19 December ("Two Directors at the Récamier for One Lorca Play") that Auclair had installed her daughter Françoise Prévost as co-director with Suarès.

When the postponed premiere finally came, critical response was harsh. While announcing an "exciting evening," G. Joly in *L'Aurore* (29 December) criticized nonetheless a lack of correspondence ("désacord") between the text and its overlavish production (Figure 2). Others were less reticent: *L'Intransigeant* (23 December) damned the "deadly boredom" of the piece, praising only Raymundo de Larrain's sumptuous decors, while *France Soir* (25 December) deplored the lack of the "common sense and clarity" once championed by Voltaire: the reviewer affects to regret that he is not one of the "morbid, neurotic intellectuals" for whom all obscurity is profound. *Le Parisien Libéré* (26 December) attacks the "preciosity" of the production, with its decadent decors that "denature" García Lorca and "pretend" to be poetic ("faire poétique"). *Les Arts* (31 December) repeats the charge of preciosity, adding that García Lorca's voice has been "suffocated" and that the production can only give ammunition to the enemies of truly "poetic theater."

Figure 2. Laurent Terzieff (Young Man, *left*) and Jean-Marie Serreau (Old Man, *right*) in *Así que pasen cinco años* (*When Five Years Have Passed*), Paris 1958.

Le Carrefour on the same date also defends the "positive avant garde" or "Left Bank" theater for which the new venue is perfectly equipped. But in this case, when play, actors, and decors are wholly disconnected, there is nothing but empty formalism. The sets and costumes are in the worst taste, recalling a detergent commercial or a drag ball *chez* Duchess Marie-Chantal (a proverbially pretentious figure). *Les Lettres Françaises* (1 January 1959) thinks the art design more appropriate for a *parfumier*'s shop window in the Faubourg Saint-Honoré than for a serious play. Most ferocious of all is Jean-Jacques Gautier in *Le Figaro* (a conservative critic who was later to attack an experimental production of *La Celestina*).[21] His piece (23 December 1958) is prefaced by a caricature that shows the audience not sitting in their seats but rather sleeping on couches, like the Fiancée at the start of Act II. Dismissing the piece as a *grimoire* (originally a magician's spell book; now any incomprehensible text), he attacks all aspects of the production, singling out the cast's delivery of the impenetrable text: "Are the actors French or foreign? Those without accents seem to be reciting a text in an unknown language. The accent of the others makes their lines unintelligible, even if they are speaking French."

It is clear, then, that *Así que pasen cinco años* was interpreted within the context of contemporary debates around Parisian theater. The first debate was economic – while critics applauded the reconversion of a cinema to drama, they wondered whether Paris could support yet another theater and predicted commercial disaster for the Récamier after this unpropitious beginning. The second debate was generic – while some critics were sympathetic to minority theater (whether they called it educational, quality, avant-garde, or Left Bank), others clearly resented the challenge to commercial criteria posed by a play that (to cite G. Joly) "violently challenges the bovine stupidity that congratulates itself on understanding nothing." But such questions of taste and intelligibility also intersected with gender, sexuality, and nationality: Raymundo de Larrain's flamboyant lace and feather designs were read as feminine or, indeed, effeminate; foreign-born cast or crew were held to be alien to familiar French notions of rationality and clarity. The *grimoire* of *Así que pasen cinco años* was a closed book to Parisians such as Claude Olivier in *Les Lettres Françaises* (1 January 1959), who saw García Lorca as "the author of *Mariana Pineda* and *Doña Rosita*." Paradoxically, critics thus resented both the "foreignness" of *Así que pasen cinco años* and its lack of that picturesque exoticism (that *espagnolade*) which they had come to expect from García Lorca. Thus Gabriel Marcel laments in *Les Nouvelles Littéraires* (22 January 1959) a production whose premature closure was so "foreseeable": "Nothing more different could be imagined from all the plays we have so loved and which established Lorca's reputation here." The play's "bloodless symbolism" is "more Germanic or Scandinavian than Spanish."

Ironically, if French drama critics clung to a reassuring faith in García Lorca's ingenuous vitalism incompatible with the supposed perverse intellectualism of *Así que pasen cinco años,* it was French scholars who first stressed the conscious elaboration to which García Lorca submitted his aesthetic ideas. Writing in 1967 (but referring to her thesis of 1953), Marie Laffranque cites García Lorca's "deliberate working through [of his ideas], his firm and wide ranging thought, . . . the decisive positions he took up, [and] his entire effort of reflection."[22] Rejecting the "narrowly literary or psycholiterary" studies that had preceded hers, Laffranque exhaustively documents García Lorca's "conscious attitude towards what he allows us to call his profession" (p. 8). García Lorca, she writes, has been little known and greatly misunderstood for many years – now the "veil" can be lifted and a "progressive elucidation" achieved (p. 9).

An impeccable scholar, Laffranque is citing the patient documentation of hitherto unexamined texts, such as the contemporary Spanish press of which she makes such painstaking use. However, the lifting of the veil and the elucidation of truth as strategies had already been compromised in France by the scandalous writings of Jean-Pierre Schonberg, alias Baron Louis Stinglhamber. Schonberg's first claim to notoriety was his claim in 1956, unsubstantiated but widely believed, that García Lorca's death was motivated not by political but rather by personal concerns – "questions de moeurs."[23] In this obscure homosexual intrigue, Schonberg cites successively as jealous rivals of García Lorca in Granada Ruiz Alonso the boorishly heterosexual Catholic of the extreme right; "Don G. M., painter of ephebes"; and the "outraged father of a wretched adolescent, initiated into vice by Lorca" (pp. 119–20). Ian Gibson has demolished Schonberg's tenuous claims to objective truth[24] (one of Schonberg's witnesses is said to be "a young English woman . . . scandalized by Lorca's strange relations with *toreros*" [p. 10]). What interests me rather is the persistence and violence of Schonberg's homosexual fantasies projected onto García Lorca and their relation to the allegorical mode in which the text must be made to say something other – the veil stripped away, the silence filled with voices (p. 7).

For Schonberg, the life is the "key" to the work, and that life is tainted by the "Corydonian shadow." Excessively docile at school, mother-fixated at home, García Lorca suffers a precocious breakdown:

Finished for ever the love for young girls, we can make out [*deviner*] in him a final crisis, of an erotic character, and feel the growth of the monster of desire which comes to meet him, pulling him along and filling him with sadness. [García Lorca is] a child who exchanges his green paradise for a season in hell. (p. 33)

Already hyperfeminine and impressionable, the now *maudit* García Lorca absorbs from Dalí the surrealist "venom which already poisoned him and was literally to destroy him . . . [García Lorca] will taste the bitter dregs of forbidden desires, inextinguishable even in abandonment and solitary pleasure" (p. 58). Or again, *Poeta en Nueva York* "lifts the veil on the scandal of the life of a satrap . . . nights in the lower depths, cheap rate sodomy, a collection of seedy partners. . . . How can we not know it all, under the cover of a falsely surreal language, necessarily hermetic? Where is his face?" (p. 84).

There are two paradoxes here. The first is that unmasking or elucidation, the stripping away of García Lorca's poetic cover, leads only to renewed obscurity – the unlocatable face of Corydonian love, resolutely hidden from the prurient but protesting Schonberg. The second is that homosexuality is at once inflated or expanded and deflated or disembodied. Schonberg claims both that homosexuality suffuses the life and work as the single key that unlocks the intolerable hermeticism of García Lorca's writing and that the same life and work are characterized by continual impotence, hesitance, and isolation. Attributing to the young García Lorca a syphilitic infection for which he offers no empirical evidence, Schonberg sacrifices historical reference on the altar of symbolic interpretation, reducing all anecdote to allegory. At its

most extreme, García Lorca's elegy on the death of Ignacio
Sánchez Mejías, a poetic response to an undeniably public event,
becomes "under the figure of Ignacio ... the drama of [García
Lorca's] own personal misadventure ... that evening when Corydon inflicted the Neapolitan pox on him ... which was to carry
him off after a long, humiliating, and terrible struggle" (p. 255).
Like the Parisian critics of *Así que pasen cinco años*, Schonberg finds
obscurity intolerable; it must be substituted by clarity and intelligibility, whatever the cost to the spirit or letter of the text. And like
modern scholars of *Así que pasen cinco años*, Schonberg cannot tolerate desiring relations between men – the external relation
between García Lorca and Sánchez Mejías becomes an internal
monologue, the other simply a narcissistic mirror of the same.

Moreover, as the homosexual has no object (García Lorca is
deprived even of his love for the dead *torero*), he can play no substantial part in the world and must be destined only for death.
Thus while Schonberg begins his study with the Terentian tag "Ve-
ritas odium parit" (meaning that his discovery of García Lorca's
"true nature" has brought him the hatred of the playwright's sup-
porters), it is not truth that gives birth to hatred, but rather hatred
to truth – it is Schonberg's hatred for homosexuals, women, and
Spaniards (the last repeatedly castigated for failing to accede to his
own Cartesian perspective)[25] that gives birth to his version of truth:
a tearing of the veil of secrecy that culpably covers the perverse, the
impressionable, and the feminized. His is a monolithic "thematic
system" characteristic of a certain strand of French criticism in the
1960s, when Jean-Paul Weber's "generalization of psychoanalysis"
claimed to find single, obsessive motifs of a sexual or infantile character throughout the lives and the works of Hugo, Vigny, and Verlaine.[26]

What, then, is Schonberg's reading of *Así que pasen cinco años?*
After citing at length Jean-Jacques Gautier's abusive notice in *Le
Figaro*, Schonberg claims that the play is by no means unintelligible
but is rather the disguised story of García Lorca's supposed impotence and syphilis, a dialogue of the poet with himself. In Act I the

Young Man is, of course, García Lorca; but the Fiancée is his penis, to whose pleasures he must bid farewell for the "medically prescribed" period of five years (p. 311). In Act II, the loss of the Fiancée (her flight with the Rugby Player) signals a renewed bout of syphilis, following a blennorrhagic (white mucus) discharge. The Mannequin represents the poet's consequent sterility. The return and loss of the Typist in Act III also signals penile inadequacy – the Young Man's life is but an empty masquerade that can culminate only in death (p. 312). *Así que pasen cinco años* is thus "the devil's box, protected by one hundred keys possessed only by those initiated into the Corydonian lexicon."

Let us compare the account of *Así que pasen cinco años* in another life and work of the poet, published in 1968 by Marcelle Auclair, who had translated the play for the ill-fated production ten years earlier.[27] Auclair places the play historically: It is to be read in the context of García Lorca's attempt to nurture an audience for yet more unplayable plays such as the previously completed *El público* (p. 232). And if, like all critics, she takes the three men of Act I (the Old Man and the two Friends) to be "varying aspects of a single man: the author himself," she problematizes that identification, citing a letter from the period in which García Lorca claims not to recognize himself in the mirror (p. 234). Then come anecdotal elements – the blue pajamas of the Young Man are those García Lorca liked to wear at home; the miniature theater of Act III is the puppet theater he loved all his life; Isabel García Lorca has given Auclair other "keys" to the play, based on infantile memories (p. 236). Finally, the Young Man's reluctance to put on new shoes in the last scene is derived from García Lorca's attachment to his own battered footwear, the symbol of his vibrantly active life (p. 239).

Auclair makes some general observations on *Así que pasen cinco años* as the play as vertigo and immobility – it is a dizzying spectacle of temporal paradox and personal splitting. But in general she refuses to make the play say other than it does, attempting rather to pin down its anecdotal referents. But those anecdotes are underwritten by testimony, Auclair's own knowledge of and continuing love for García Lorca: "When his friends and I meet once more, at first I see on their faces wrinkles which would have been his. Only at first: they seem to melt away as soon as we speak of what we lived with him. Federico is our youth" (p. 238). Unlike Schonberg's violent interpretation, then, Auclair's authoritative testimony is not solitary but communal; each surviving witness recognizes in the other the traces of the time that has passed since they knew the mourned person, traces that are etched in their faces. Testimony thus both transcends time and bears witness to its passing, a theme shared by *Así que pasen cinco años* itself – the Young Man is terrified by the appearance of two tiny wrinkles in his Fiancée's face (I, p. 204).

However, the anecdotal method can also be violently reductive. Taking on Schonberg explicitly for once, Auclair ridicules his "pseudo-Freudian" reading of the poem "Son de negros en Cuba." Where Schonberg takes "the blond head of Fonseca" to be the "dry fountain" of García Lorca's sterile sex and reads a reference to Romeo and Juliet as a male couple in the style of *El público*, Auclair identifies the images as labels on Cuban cigar boxes: "In the presence of the sources [of the poem] it is amusing to see a critic's sexual obsession exert itself over this text. . . . Could Señor Fonseca have imagined that the ravishing decoration of his cigar boxes could give rise to such pseudo-Freudian tampering with the text ['tripatouillage']? . . . As always, Lorca is describing" (p. 429).

But description cannot account for the connotative value of poetry; reference cannot exhaust resonance. And the case of homosexuality is once more one that "description" cannot address. Thus Auclair insists, against Schonberg, that García Lorca's homosexuality was simply "anecdotal," that it bore no particular significance in relation to his work (p. 104); and recalling García Lorca's easy and frequent laughter, she dismisses any frustrations he may have felt at his supposed sterility, while stressing the virulent homophobia of the "Spanish context" in which García Lorca lived (p. 108). Skeptical of literary uses of psychoanalysis and dismissive of the "temptation to seek the psychoanalytic meaning of [poetic] images" (p. 88), Auclair cannot explain why friends such as herself could be intimate with García Lorca for years without having the slightest awareness of his homosexuality (p. 194). And yet she tells us of evenings when García Lorca would delight the company after dinner with improvised performances dressed as Mata Hari (p. 201). While the allegorical obsessive presses into service the most unlikely details to serve his totalizing interpretation, the anecdotal witness cannot raise incidents to the level of ideas or integrate the specific event of a friend's masquerade within the general concept of homosexuality.

Moreover, the testimony on which Auclair's book relies is inherently, movingly fragile – the one photo of Auclair and García Lorca together is hopelessly blurred (still she reproduces it in her book); the day when García Lorca read *Bodas de sangre* to fellow guests at Marañón's country estate, the playwright asked Auclair not to take so many photographs of him. The pictures she did take subsequently "took flight" and were reproduced without permission elsewhere (opposite p. 312). An enduring testimony to time and to friendship, Auclair's work is also a troubling reminder of the implication of the witness in the scene she observes and of the fragility of life histories that are not simply dialogues with oneself but are rather (like the analysand's anamnesis) remade in collaboration with others.

3. Corydon: Gender, Nature, History

Ian Gibson cites the one letter to have survived from Rafael Rodríguez Rapún to García Lorca, written on 12 October 1933.[28] It confesses Rodríguez Rapún's longing for García Lorca while they are separated and his constant remembering of the time they have spent together. Rodríguez Rapún has been cast as the rustic fisherman in La Barraca's production of Tirso's *El burlador de Sevilla*, a character by the name of "Coridón." He adds: "according to [mutual friend Eduardo] Ugarte I am a 'Coridón' in the good sense of the word." As Gibson remarks, the reference is to Gide's early apology for homosexuality, *Corydon*, first published in Spanish four years earlier, in 1929.

Gibson goes on to lament the loss of García Lorca's personal letters, which, he claims, combined with "the poet's own discretion

have contrived to make [his private life] at times almost impenetrable" (p. 361). It is possible, however, to respect the reticence of
Rodríguez Rapún and García Lorca (their discreet classical cod-
ing) and pick up on their mutual reference without violently pen-
etrating their intimacy. It is a reticence and a hesitance that Gide
himself felt toward *Corydon*, whose publication he delayed by ten
years after its composition. If I argue, then, for a Gidian rereading
of García Lorca it is analogous to my appeal to Freud in the same
context – neither an insistence on influence, nor a turning of the
key of interpretation, but rather an attention to the structural similarity of one work to the other.[29] It remains the case, however, that
the opening predicament of *Corydon* is strikingly similar to that of
Así que pasen cinco años – the unnamed narrator has a rendezvous
with the friend he has not seen for a specified period, in this case
ten years (p. 15).[30] Corydon's is the story of a postponed engagement and a missed encounter with a woman:

> I lived with the obsession of marrying a young girl . . . who I loved at
> that time more than anything in the world. I loved her too much to
> realize that I did not desire her. . . . Attempting to persuade myself of
> the merit of my abstinence, I exalted at the idea of coming to marriage
> as a virgin. . . . Melancholy clouded my life . . . and being unable to
> admit to my fiancée anything of the causes of my sadness, my attitude
> towards her became increasing equivocal and awkward. . . . I believed
> myself to be incapable of desire. (pp. 27–8)

This delay and lack of desire, this problematic relation to the
betrothed, is precisely that of the Young Man at the start of Act I,
who has suspended his engagement "for reasons that are not to be
explained" ("Por cosas que no son de explicar"; p. 196); who cannot use the word "fiancée" without seeing his "little girl" "shrouded
in the sky" ("muchachita . . . amortajada en [el] cielo"; p. 201); and
who would like to desire a woman "as [he] would like to be thirsty
before a fountain" ("Yo quisiera quererla como quisiera tener sed
delante de las fuentes"; p. 209). Corydon's "mystical" love for the
fiancée (his missed encounter with the woman) gives way to a proposal from another. But it is not García Lorca's Typist but rather the
fiancée's adolescent brother, Alexis, who requests physical intimacy

with him (p. 32). Refusing reciprocity (as the Young Man refuses the Typist), Corydon resists the youth's repeated requests and "exaggerates [his] coldness towards him" (p. 32). The tragic result is the definitive loss of the love object – the youth commits suicide, a "drama" that "finally opens [Corydon's] eyes to [him]self" (p. 35).

Abandoning the "comedy" of his engagement (p. 28) and adopting the less accustomed role of the masculine-identified pederast, Corydon claims to have achieved a self-realization of which García Lorca's Young Man appears to be incapable. Yet *Corydon* shares the curious combination of vertigo and immobility with *Así que pasen cinco años*. Thus, after this prologue of successive postponements (by Gide, by the narrator, and by Corydon), the two participants in the dialogue return repeatedly to the hermetic space of Corydon's "austere" apartment, as isolated from the chaos of life as is the Young Man's library. Yet the dialogue form implies a splitting of subjectivity, which gives free play to Gide's habitual irony, even here where he aims for "serious thought" and scorns the pleasures of art and wit (p. 12). Homophobic, misogynistic, and anti-Semitic, the narrator hardly cuts an attractive figure as he demands his former friend's "confession" (26); but Corydon himself with his dryly scientific tone and "affectation of severity" in dress and manner (p. 16) is scarcely seductive. And as we shall see, the dialogue ends in a resounding silence that resists interpretation.

If *Corydon* foreshadows in a very different register the temporal, spatial, and subjective doublings of *Así que pasen cinco años,* the dialogue also gives willfully perverse accounts of gender, nature, and history that enable a productive rereading of the play. Thus Gide admits an infinite variety of uranism: "Homosexuality, just like heterosexuality, includes all degrees: from Platonism to salaciousness, from self-denial to sadism, . . . from the simplest of expressions to all the refinements of vice" (p. 36). Just so, the Young Man's inexplicable chastity gives way to the urgent and ambiguous demands of the First Friend, who spins around with the Young Man in his arms, rubs noses with him, takes his head between his legs, and drunkenly announces that a woman can be frightfully ugly and a male horse tamer beautiful (I, p. 213). He is followed by the Second Friend, feminine identified in his "impeccable" white suit, gloves, and shoes and his curly lace tie, whom García Lorca tells us should be played by "a very young actor or a girl" ("un actor muy joven [o] una muchacha"; I, p. 235). The epitome of infantile regression as well as effeminacy, the Second Friend curls up fetally on the sofa and falls asleep at the end of the Act (I, p. 244). Characters, then, who have always been taken as representing distinct modes of time (present and past, respectively), the two friends also embody two modes of homosexuality in the Gidian style – virile salaciousness and pitiful, plaintive inversion (p. 36).

This cult of the male recurs in Gide's (or rather Corydon's) account of the dimorphic sex system in the natural world – the male role is that of massive and frequently fruitless expenditure, the female that of passive accumulation (p. 70). Problematic here, however (and relevant for *Así que pasen cinco años*), is the question of choice – while in the animal kingdom it is the female that chooses the male, in human society the reverse is the case; moreover, while animals can mate only periodically, human desire is in constant operation (p. 118). So-called sexual instinct is thus "undecided," prone to reversal and intermittence in both sexes (p. 102). Similarly in García Lorca, indecision is combined with inversion – the Young Man, hesitating over his choice of the Fiancée, is then rejected by the Fiancée, who herself chooses the unequivocally masculine Rugby Player; the Typist, who at first chose the Young Man, later rejects him when he chooses her, opting for continuing indecision. This "reversal of affect" (in Freud's phrase) can thus be read not simply as an idiosyncrasy of García Lorca's characters but rather (with Gide) as a testimony to the fundamental lack of physical reciprocity and temporal coincidence between males and females in Nature – masculine desire is a game of chance played "hors des règles" ("without rules," but also "outside of [the periodic rhythm] of menstruation," p. 117).

If Gide, then, like García Lorca appeals frequently to the example of animals (and most generally invertebrates, such as insects and mollusks), then he does so with perverse intent – to demonstrate the superfluity of the male, who is but a sport or a snack to the female of the species (most spectacularly in the case of the praying mantis). In the absence of a sexual instinct (which was

invented simply as a substitute for the dead divinity, pp. 53, 74),
beasts and men strive only for pleasure, with fertilization nothing
but a *raccroc* – a lucky stroke in the game of sexual billiards (p. 59).

García Lorca appears at first sight to reject this downgrading of
reproduction in the face of the more urgent demands of pleasure
– the Fiancée hears the cry of a child among the mirrors and laces
of her bedroom ("En los espejos y entre los encajes de la cama oigo
ya el gemido de un niño que me persigue"; II, p. 270); the Mannequin calls out to a phantom child, lost offspring of the aborted
wedding ("Mi hijo.¡Quiero a mi hijo!"; II, p. 283); even the Young
Man feels a son stir within him, "like a little ant alone in a closed
box" ("Corre por dentro de mí, como una hormiguita sola dentro
de una caja cerrada"; III, 1, p. 322). With this final fantasy of male
pregnancy, however (to which I return in the section on Freud,
which follows this one), García Lorca effects, like Gide in his very
different way, a rupture between desire and reproduction, between
sexual instinct and its "natural" (heterosexual) object.

This inversion or reversion is clearer in Gide's account of the
tricky text of Nature:

Nature forms a network without beginning or end, an uninterrupted
sequence of links which it is impossible to know which way to get hold
of; and nothing is more problematic than knowing if each of the links
has its purpose in the one which precedes or follows it . . . and if the
whole book of Nature, in order to be properly understood, should not
be read back to front – that is to say, if the last page is not the explanation of the first, and the last link the secret motive for the beginning. . . . (p. 79)

Gide is writing here in the technical context of the debate between
Evolutionists and Finalists, who (he claims) meet at the same
point, although they follow their respective paths in opposite
directions (p. 81). But the endless, reversible chain is a fine image
of the complex model of temporality and causality in *Así que pasen
cinco años*, which begins with the Old Man's defiant assertion that
we should "remember towards tomorrow" (I, p. 194). Chronological confusion can thus be read as a refutation of the certainties of

gender and nature, which may be reversed or inverted at any point in the endless chain of links of which they are composed.

Proclaiming the naturalness of homosexuality, Gide goes on, perversely once more, to challenge received notions of history – periods in which pederasty flourished are those of cultural efflorescence, not decadence. Abandoning the insects and mollusks, Corydon extolls the glories of ancient Athens and Renaissance Florence, their cultural treasures inseparable ("like a flower on the plant that supports it") from the pederasty underlying them (p. 154). The decadence of art begins with the admission of women as objects of desire, as when pastoral poetry became "an apprenticeship in heterosexuality" (p. 138). At this point Corydon's interlocutor intervenes, citing the reciprocal desire between male and female lovers, which requires no effort of literary imitation (pp. 139–40). But Corydon counters, citing Virgil's Eclogue III, in which the shepherdess flees from her suitor while two shepherds enjoy a "pleasure without reticence" (p. 141).

Curiously, in the abstracted world of *Así que pasen cinco años*, the few concrete cultural references in the text are also to Italy and to antiquity – the Yellow Mask's tale of her lost love is spoken with an Italian accent; and the mysteriously theatrical wood of Act III invokes the equally self-conscious landscape of classical pastoral. Moreover, there is here an explicit if enigmatic reference to Virgil, author of Eclogue II, from which Gide's names Corydon and Alexis derive:

ARLEQUÍN: (Enfático) El poeta Virgilio construyó una mosca de oro y murieron todas las moscas que envenenaban el aire de Nápoles: ahí dentro en el circo hay oro blando, suficiente para hacer una estatua del mismo tamaño . . . que usted. (III, p. 310, footnote)
HARLEQUIN: (Forcefully) The poet Virgil made a gold fly and all the flies that were poisoning the air of Naples died: in there in the circus there is soft gold, enough to make a statue the same size . . . as you.

This anecdote (omitted from Ucelay's text) reveals the complex process of condensation in García Lorca's oblique classical references. I have already suggested that the theatrical forest is the equivalent of the stylized pastoral *locus amoenus,* in which death is also always present. The reference to a "golden fly," however, recalls Virgil's Georgics IV, devoted to bees and their liquid gold. Moreover, the deadly solipsism of the Young Man, suggested by the Harlequin's insinuation that he should make a statue of himself, also has a precedent in the Georgics where Virgil's bees, like García Lorca's chaste Young Man, "do not engage in intercourse, nor wear out their bodies in sexual love [*in Venerem*] . . . but rather gather up their new born themselves in their mouths from leaves and sweet herbs" (198–201). If Virgil's bees are thus one precedent for the Young Man's fantasy of asexual reproduction, a further precedent emerges – in the "Culex," an early poem traditionally attributed to Virgil, the gnat of the title, killed by a shepherd, returns to tell him of the horrors of the underworld, foreshadowing the Dead Cat's lament in Act I.[31]

Pace Gide, then, pastoral is not always an exemplum of homosexual reciprocity, of sexual practice without reticence; indeed, Virgil's original Corydon laments throughout Eclogue II the indifference of his beloved Alexis. But this indecision of the love object is echoed in Gide's final proposition of the proper relation between the adult pedagogue and the youthful subject of his sentimental education: "the appetite which awakes in the adolescent is not born of a specific demand. . . . [I]t is rare for his desire to be defined by itself without the aid of experience" (p. 146); or again:

His desire is shifting and remains at the mercy of external impressions. . . . Until the age of about eighteen he inspires love more than he knows how to love himself. . . . More desirable and desired than desiring he is guided by his lover towards those radiant peaks which cannot be reached without love. If this adolescent falls into the hands of a woman, he may come to a sticky end. (pp. 181–2)

The fragility of the Young Man's desire, his indecision and abulia, are here recast in the context of a pseudo-Hellenic erotic pedagogy – not so much Corydon as Alexis, if he does not know himself what he wants, then surely Gide will tell him.

It is precisely this vulnerability and indecision that Gregorio

Marañón seeks to protect and to preserve in his "anti-Socratic" dialogue on *Corydon:*

This age [of adolescence], which is dangerous because of natural law, must be rigorously watched over by the pedagogue . . . in order to assist [the adolescent] with a virile staff to pass through it austerely, sublimating his indecisive sexuality and storing it up for the future in an aseptic chamber, where it is embalmed in fertile physical exhaustion, in wondrous hopes, and in an austere morality bordering on aridity. To make of this perilous transition a sexual object is monstrous. (Spanish translation, pp. 21–2)

There could be no finer description of the Young Man's predicament – his austerity and indecision lead him to postpone desire and to embalm himself in the hermetically sealed space of the library. But, as Marañón's own rhetoric suggests in spite of itself, such a strategy can lead only to death. Similarly, even Gide's praise of efflorescent male play admits that "the prestigious means of seduction" such as butterflies' wings or birds' feathers are but "a vain display of dead [body] parts" (p. 73). And just as *Así que pasen cinco años* ends with an all-male card game in which the Young Man is mocked by an Echo repeating his last words, so *Corydon* closes with the narrator's resonant and irrefutable silence: "Without adding anything but a farewell I took my hat and left, in the knowledge that some arguments are better answered by a good silence than by anything one might find to say" (p. 183).

4. Fragments of an Analysis

Freud's famous case history of Dora ("Fragment of an Analysis of a Case of Hysteria"), a narrative of whose literary quality he himself is cautiously aware (p. 94),[32] reproduces narrative elements that should be familiar by now – multiple postponements, rejected proposals, and the deferral of a marriage. Thus Freud himself delays publication of the case for a period of five years (from 1900 to 1905) and on more than one occasion misassigns his treatment to the wrong year. But Dora also delays – rejecting (inexplicably to Freud [p. 70]) the sexual proposal of Herr K., a handsome married friend of her father's, she at first neglects to inform her parents of this incident ("the scene by the lake") and of an earlier scene ("the scene of the kiss") in which, Freud speculates, Herr K. had pressed his erect penis against the fifteen-year-old girl's body. But marriage must be ever deferred – claiming Dora hopes to marry Herr K. after he has divorced his wife (although Herr K.'s "proposal" to Dora [p. 134] is by no means of the matrimonial kind), Freud adds to the cast of characters a young man who "intended to come forward as a [Dora's] suitor one day. . . . But that would take time and it meant waiting" (p. 135). The "fantasy of waiting for a fiancé" is thus said to be a founding moment of Dora's self-narrative.

As in *Así que pasen cinco años*, then, there is thus a staggering of heterosexual desire that remains resolutely nonreciprocal – just as García Lorca's Young Man rejects the Typist, only to be rejected in turn by her, so Dora rejects Herr K., only to be offended by his subsequent lack of attention; she feels she has been treated like a governess. And if the leisured milieu of the case history is reminiscent of the bourgeois setting of *Así que pasen cinco años*'s relatively naturalistic Act II (with its father, daughter, suitor, and servant), then the psychopathology of Freud's cast of characters also anticipates García Lorca's. The Young Man and the Typist reveal "one of the most essential features of a neurosis": "[the] incapacity for meeting a real erotic demand. . . . If what [neurotics] long for most intensely in their fantasies is presented them in reality, they . . . flee from it" (p. 151). Or again, ever defensive against the noise and dirt of the street that cannot be allowed to penetrate his house, the Young Man coincides with the cleaning fetish or "housewife's psychosis" of Dora's mother, which Freud attributes to the syphilitic infection and discharge communicated to her (and hence to Dora) by her subsequently impotent father (p. 49). Finally, like Little Hans (the object of Freud's next case history), the Young Man might be read as a phobic: "erecting mental barriers in the nature of precautions, inhibitions, or prohibitions" (p. 275); "protective structures" through which "pleasure [is] transformed into anxiety" (p. 276).

More important than these symptoms (which in both García Lorca and Freud are distributed among the characters of their respective narratives and whose meaning is simply "soldered together" with the symptom [p. 73]) is the question of the periodicity of time. Thus "the length of [Dora's] attacks would remain as a trace of their original significance" (i.e., their precipitating cause in the real [p. 71]); "miraculous" analytical cures occur after "some stated period of time has elapsed" (p. 78); or again, citing Dora's "fantasy of childbirth" (which occurred nine months after "the scene by the lake"), Freud claims that "periods of time are never a matter of indifference" (p. 143). Fusing simultaneity and sequentiality, other patients such as Anna O. "relive [in sequence] the previous year" (*Studies on Hysteria*, p. 87). A more specific antecedent to the play, Mathilde H. suffered from a depression caused by "the breaking off of her engagement, which had occurred several months earlier. . . . She had fallen into a state of indecision . . . and every day she was possessed by the mood and thought which were appropriate to the day in the past with which she was occupied" (*Studies on Hysteria*, p. 234, footnote). The case histories thus exhibit that curious combination of vertigo and immobility so characteristic of *Así que pasen cinco años*'s compulsive repetitions.

But it is at a structural level that play and anamnesis coincide most closely. Freud repeatedly stresses that his analysis of Dora is fragmentary – first, "everything . . . emerges piecemeal, woven into various contexts, and distributed over widely separated periods of time" (p. 41); second, he has "not reproduced the process of interpretation . . . only the results of that process"; finally, a single case history cannot prove the psychosexual etiology of all cases of hysteria (p. 42). These three kinds of fragmentation have two further consequences. The first is the demand for yet another postponement – the skeptic should "suspend his judgment" (p. 42), just as the analyst must defer interpretation. The second is the "theoretical significance" of the fragment – "the patients' inability to give an ordered history of their life" is not accidental but rather inextricably related to their condition (p. 41). The primacy of the fragment further implies a bias toward contiguity: "an internal connection which is still undisclosed will announce its presence by means of a contiguity – a temporal proximity – of associations; just as in writing if 'a' and 'b' are put side by side, it means that the syllable 'ab' is formed" (p. 71). It is a technique exploited by the apparently random juxtaposition of scenes in *Así que pasen cinco años*, when, say, the Dead Cat and Child are made to be temporally proximate (contiguous) with the Old and Young Men of Act I. Contiguity thus suggests (but does not resolve) connections whose significance (like that of the enigmatic syllable "ab") must be postponed for a specific but indefinite period of time. Such relations are, like the "associative chains" in the case of Little Hans, "pliable and ambiguous," subject to "distortion and substitution" (pp. 293, 294).

The logic of the fragment also implies a recursive or inverted chronology: Dora's "scene by the lake" is revealed before the "scene of the kiss" in Herr K.'s workplace, which, nonetheless, preceded it (p. 58); in Hans's horse phobia "what emerges from the unconscious is to be understood in the light not of what goes before but what comes after" (p. 227). Remembering "toward the future" (like García Lorca's Old Man), Freud's hysterics reverse the sequence of cause and effect "through a chain of intermediate causal links" (*Studies on Hysteria*, p. 58) that "are given in a reverse chronological order" (*Studies on Hysteria*, p. 134).

But this temporal technique is also affective and somatic – through the "reversal of affect" (p. 49) and the "displacement of sensation" (p. 61), excitement becomes disgust and genital stimulation an irritation of the throat. Displacing the lower part of the body to the upper, Dora displays in her nervous cough the "disgust [that] clings to sexual life and cannot be detached from it in spite of every effort at idealization" (p. 63). The Young Man's hysterical unsociability and *taedium vitae* (symptoms also shared by Dora [p. 54]) likewise testify, albeit obliquely, to the three determinants of hysteria – psychic trauma, conflict of affects, and disturbance in the sphere of sexuality.

However, to borrow a theatrical metaphor from Freud himself, "sexuality does not simply intervene [in the anamnesis], like a deus ex machina" (p. 156). And if the symptoms constitute the patient's

sexual activity, then that activity is the result of a complex inter-
weaving of memory and fantasy – the dream stands "on two legs"
("the current exciting cause" and a childhood trauma), and the
wish behind the dream is to "summon childhood back into reality
and correct the present day by the measure of childhood" (p. 107).

García Lorca's characters, then, are like Freud's hysterics who,
famously, "suffer from reminiscences" (*Studies on Hysteria,* p. 58).
They remain tormented by memories such as the Typist's vision of
the Young Man's youthful fall and bloodied knee – "a red snake
trembling between my breasts" ("una sierpe roja temblando entre
mis pechos"; I, 208). But that infantile sexuality is not simply
recalled but is rather acted out in the allegorical figures of the
drama. Thus the Dead Child and Cat of Act II give direct voice to
the sexual theories of children that Freud found confirmed in Little Hans – the Child continues to attribute a penis to the Cat even
after she has informed him she is a girl; and he fears their "willies"
("cucas") will be eaten by lizards when they are buried (I, 226).
The allegorical pair thus reconfirm Freud's hypothesis of the
"homosexuality" of children (who recognize only one sexual
organ) and the universality of the castration complex (pp. 198,
268).

However, these infantile theories recur elsewhere in *Así que
pasen cinco años,* emerging (in Freud's words) "piecemeal, woven
into various contexts, and distributed over widely separated periods of time." Thus the fantasy of pregnancy (including the male
pregnancy Freud notes in Hans [pp. 241, 254]) is attributed in
turn to the Second Friend in Act I, who nurtures a "tiny woman" in
a drop of water ("una de esas mujercillas de la lluvia"; p. 236); to
the Maid in Act II, who claims her father was so small he traveled
to Brazil "inside a suitcase" ("Era tan chico que cabía en una
maleta"; p. 253); and to the Young Man in Act III, who (as we have
already seen) proclaims the presence of an antlike child inside his
body (p. 227). The symptom is thus split in a *condition seconde*[33]
across multiple characters. Similarly, the symbolic geography of
the dream (Dora's sexual topography of forest–pubic hair and

woodland-nymphae) is reproduced in García Lorca's mysterious forest of Act III whose "great tree trunks" ("grandes troncos"; p. 292), however, resist reduction to any single referent.

This brings us to the final and most puzzling characteristic of Dora's life history – its multiple and simultaneous identifications, as complex as those in García Lorca's drama. Thus Dora "puts herself in her mother's place" as her father's lover; and "in Frau K.'s place" as the (unconsciously cathected) admirer of Herr K. whose proposal she had so violently rejected (p. 90). Or again, like the lovesick governess who used Dora as a way to reach her father, so (according to Freud at least) Dora used Herr K.'s children to reach their father (p. 68). It is a vertiginous sequence analogous to the failed encounters of *Así que pasen cinco años* – the Young Man rejects the Typist's proposal in Act I, just as she will reject his in Act III. Moreover, and less obviously, the male Servant of Act I is replaced by the Maid in Act II, who performs the same action of lighting the lamp; or again, in a little-discussed scene in Act III, the Typist and the Mask repeat to each other lines first spoken in Act I by the Young and Old Men. What is suggested by García Lorca's repetitions in a different place is that if heterosexual desire remains eternally nonreciprocal, then cross-gender identification is nevertheless inevitable – the Servant becomes the Maid, and the two austere Men become the extravagantly feminine Mask and the Typist.

However, what García Lorca does not represent in *Así que pasen cinco años* (although he does in *El público*) is an overtly homosexual relation. This repressed relation is split between two characters whom critics have not, to my knowledge, ever thought to identify – the Young Man and his Fiancée. Thus the Young Man represents a masculine identification whose desire has no object, and the Fiancée a feminine identification whose masculine object choice remains quite literally unresponsive (the Rugby Player stays mute throughout her ardent profession of love). Desiring but undesired, central to the opening scenes of their successive Acts, the Young Man and the Fiancée are placed side by side in a relation of contiguity (like that between the letters of "a" and "b") whose connection cannot yet be disclosed but only projected into the indefinitely postponed time frame of an "unplayable play" – the "theater of the future."[34]

In Freud also, male-identified desire and male-identified object are irreconcilable, at least in the version of homosexual etiology we are given for Little Hans – the homosexual will fix his libido upon the "woman with a penis," a "youth of feminine appearance"; or again, homosexuals "have remained fixated at a point between [autoerotism and object-love] . . . a point which is closer to auto-eroticism" (p. 268). The distant relative of Schonberg's pathologi-cally narcissistic Corydon or, indeed, Gide's indifferently receptive adolescent, the Freudian homosexual has not "found his way to [an] object love" (p. 269), which is assumed to be exclusively het-erosexual; inversely but consistently, Dora's final capitulation to marriage is heralded triumphantly but implausibly by Freud as her being "reclaimed by the realities of life" (p. 164).

But just as García Lorca's critics dare not consider the Young Man's identification with the Fiancée, so (as commentators have frequently noted) Freud cannot bear to dwell on either Dora's les-bian love for Frau K., which he himself cites as the "single simple factor . . . behind [Dora's] almost limitless series of displacements" (p. 145, footnote); or on her placing of him in the feminine posi-tion. Thus Freud relates Dora's cough to fantasized fellatio with her impotent father, rather than the more obvious option of cunnilin-gus with the "adorable" Frau K., with whom Dora shares a bed; and Dora breaks off her fragmented analysis by giving Freud two weeks' notice, thus treating him like a governess. Just as Dora's hysteria reduces her (like García Lorca's Young Man) to abulia and paraly-sis, so Freud's encounter with homosexuality "brought [him] to a standstill" (p. 162, footnote).

As beautiful and as sterile as "double flowers" (*Hysteria,* p. 321), still hysterics and homosexuals manage to reproduce. While Gar-cía Lorca's Young Man at no point shares the stage with the Rugby Player and thus cannot choose a masculine correspondent for his "love without object" ("amor sin objeto"; II, p. 272), in later life Dora and Frau K. were bridge partners in Vienna, "finally dis-pens[ing] with the superfluous men" who had engaged them and

"retain[ing] their love of those games whose skill lies in the secret
of mutual understanding of open yet coded communications."[35]
The bridge party is an alternative, upbeat ending for the homosexual relation to the downbeat final scene of *Así que pasen cinco
años*. Here the Young Man is mortally wounded at an all male card
game heavy with coded communications – to play hearts (to speak
the truth of the life) is inevitably, irredeemably, to die.

5. *From the Truth of the Life to the Life of the Truth*

Así que pasen cinco años was first performed in Spain in Miguel Narros's production at Madrid's Teatro Eslava in 1978. Drama critics
faithfully toed the academic line of interpretation, claiming, like
Manuel Gómez Ortiz in *Ya*, that the Young Man is Federico and the
action of the play is composed of his "internal monologue" ([no day
given] September 1978) or, like the anonymous critic of *ABC*, that
it depicts his "vertiginous introspections" (22 September 1978). *Ya*
draws attention to a feature of José Hernández's set design that is
relevant in this context – "tall cylinders which are [reminiscent of]
tombs, chimneys, cerebral convolutions, skyscrapers, cypresses,
with men standing on top of them like statues, men who start into
movement when it is their turn to do so, men who exist and do not
exist." The supposed unity of the action is thus reinforced by the
flexible but single decor.

Critics inevitably stress the belatedness of the production, citing
the almost half a century that elapsed since the play's composition.
And if they can no longer say, with Marcelle Auclair, "Federico is
our youth" they invoke a shared experience of loss – even Gómez
Ortiz in the rightist *Ya* begins by confessing that his desire to see
Así que pasen cinco años performed has lasted since he first read the
play as a twenty-year-old in the 1950s. A kind of historical and cultural suspension has now been brought to a close. Enrique Llovet,
writing on 21 September 1978 in *El País*, the new newspaper of the
fragile democracy, begins: "the difficult, delicate, and delayed integration of Federico García Lorca's work into the framework of our
contemporary theater now reaches its culmination and its closure
['cerramiento'] with the premiere, forty seven years after it was

written, of *Así que pasen cinco años.*" The "enormity" of the delay
does, however, have its compensations – now we can see the total-
ity of the experience of this difficult work and "the whole existence
of a character" (the Young Man). As the headline puts it: "Lorca,
All Lorca in One Play."[36]

When Narros restaged his production some ten years later at the
Teatro Español ("two periods of five years," said the critics, suggesting, like Freud, that no period of time was indifferent), the
reaction was more muted. Lorenzo López Sancho notes in *ABC*
(30 April 1989) that, in a process of repetition and substitution,
some of the cast recurs, but playing different roles from the previous production – thus Carlos Hipólito has shifted from Harlequin
to Young Man; Melio Pedregal, from Clown to Old Man. Yet others, the critic notes, have been "devoured by time." The set design
and performance style have also changed: Andrea d'Odorico's lavish sets (Figure 3) "break the spatial unity" of the piece; the dialogue is "shouted" rather than spoken with the respect due its "subtle shading" ("texto matizado"); finally, the Italian-accented mask
becomes in Manuela Vargas's performance a grotesquely distorted
("esperpéntica") Andaluza. The production thus "deuniversalizes"
the play, "leading it toward the aestheticizing *españolada.*"

Eduardo Haro Tecglen concurs in *El País* (30 April 1989), in a
notice entitled "Too Much" ("Demasiado"). While, unlike López
Sancho, he is unconcerned with the "fidelity" of the production to
the play or playwright (a question that he rightly considers "speculative" and "vain"), he finds everything excessive – the intensity of
color, violence of sound, lushness of costume, and brilliance of
lighting (this last by José Miguel López Sáez, who, Haro Tecglen
tells us, came on stage after the premiere to take a bow). Moving
from "a theater of text to a theater of spectacle," this is director's
theater with a vengeance – direction, decor, costume, effects, and
lighting are dominant, with García Lorca serving simply as a name
before the title. Noting Narros's distinguished career as a director,
Haro Tecglen claims that this is "more Narros than ever. Perhaps,
also, too much so." Like the Parisian critics of thirty years before,
then, Spaniards bemoan the excesses of this staging of *Así que pasen
cinco años;* and both groups of critics, from their very different

Figure 3. Cristina Marcos (Fiancée) in *Así que pasen cinco años* (*When Five Years Have Passed*), Madrid 1989.

times and places, situate that excess in the ambiguous realm, so
characteristic of approaches to García Lorca, between abstraction
and folklore, universality and *españolada*.

Productions of *Así que pasen cinco años* thus seem to have a tendency toward performative excess, perhaps prompted by the trou-
bling hermeticism of the text. It is tempting here to make a connection with Gide's insistence on the superfluity of the male, who
represents that parade or spectacle, irreducible to reproduction,
that (Gide claims) is the origin of both art and play.[37] Indeed,
there is evidence for such a view in García Lorca himself. Refuting
critical insistence on the supposed sterility of homosexuality,
Auclair quotes a conversation with the poet and Rodríguez Rapún
in which García Lorca praises the superiority of those who create
art over those who simply procreate (p. 111). If we should reject
that tendency to misogyny explicit in Gide's treatise and implicit in
García Lorca's reported conversation, then still the male (the
homosexual) supplement stands as a salutary corrective to that
quest for the sexual essence of the subject we find in Schonberg's
lethal "Corydonianism" and Gibson's attempt to penetrate the private – a less prurient ambition, perhaps, but equally misguided.

We have seen that in Freud the homosexual stands suspended
or paralyzed between autoeroticism and object love. I suggest that
the constant critical insistence that *Así que pasen cinco años* is a
monologue and that its action is interiorized betrays a panic about
the simple possibility of sexual relations between men that is itself
underwritten by vulgarized psychoanalytic notions of homosexuality as narcissism. If we read the monologue as dialogue (Socratic or
otherwise) and if we read sterile interiority as a fruitful relation to
the other (a relation that is perhaps confirmed by the fantasies of
procreation distributed throughout the play), then we would no
longer collude with the mortal silence and solitude in which the
Young Man, like the Director of *El público*, is condemned to death.
Virgil's Eclogue III, the "amoebean" song in which two shepherds
sing alternately the pleasures of both homo- and heterosexual love,
stands as a classical model for such a dialogue, and one that the

García Lorca who cited so obliquely the name of Virgil may well have found sympathetic.

Rejected by the Fiancée, the Young Man cries: "You are nothing. You mean nothing. My treasure is lost. My love has no object" ("Tú no eres nada. Tú no significas nada. Es mi tesoro perdido. Es mi amor sin objeto"; II, pp. 271–2). This lost treasure might be read as Freud reads the jewel case in Dora's first dream, as the precious gift of the female genitals (p. 105). But it might also be seen as the "priceless though mutilated" object of analysis, a relic of past psychic time retrieved by the patient labor of the archaeologist (p. 41). Faced with such valuable but imponderable objects, we can only defer meaning and not impose retrospectively an allegorical solution. Those critics who have insisted on turning the key of interpretation bear no relation to the Freud who insisted always on the role of condensation in the oneiric image. Thus, to take a motif familiar to García Lorca scholars, the black and white horses that are the precipitating cause (but not the simple or single origin) of Little Hans's phobia are at once the adored mother whose childbirth preceded the horses' fall; the envied and loved father whose black moustache is a bridle; and the Hans himself who took such pleasure in movement ("I am a young horse"; p. 286). This plurality of identifications, simultaneous and sequential, so similar to those in Dora's case, requires extreme circumspection from any proponent of literary or psychic analysis. Moreover, the hermeticism of *Así que pasen cinco años*'s image repertoire suggests, paradoxically, that any hard distinction between real and symbolic is impossible to sustain – as feminist commentators have noted, when Freud claims to speak plainly ("J'appelle un chat un chat"; p. 82) he not only retreats into his non-native French; he also invokes, all unknowingly, a popular figurative name for the female genitalia.[38] If, then, I began this chapter by opposing anecdote and allegory, reference and resonance, I end by stressing the fragility of the boundary between literal and symbolic, a boundary that both biographers and literary critics have so great an investment in preserving.

There is thus something to be said in favor of reticence. We have seen reticence in the brief, vertiginous dance of the Young Man and the First Friend; in Rodríguez Rapún's coded, classical allusion; in Marcelle Auclair's discreet refusal to impose meaning on the homosexuality she both saw and did not see; and (at its best) in Freud's analytical two-step, in which the analyst walks backward in front of the analysand until both come to rest in the same place, albeit by following different routes. Even the aesthetic austerity of Gide's Corydon might serve as a lesson to French and to Spanish directors of *Así que pasen cinco años,* wallowing in the extravagance of the spectacle. In reticence we find the productivity of a postponement that is at once literary, hermeneutic, and libidinal. Reticence and postponement stake out the place (the time) of an elliptical drama without clear connections between its various fragments; of a meticulous interpretation that will be tolerant of unintelligibility; and of an intermittent desire whose goal lies tensely and tenderly suspended between autoeroticism and object love.

García Lorca did not tell us his life story; and it would be naïve to think that the publication of more missing personal letters, or indeed more hitherto hidden manuscripts, would allow us to penetrate that mystery or fill its ever-yawning gap. However, the persistent desire to read *Así que pasen cinco años* as a disguised autobiography responds to the fragmented nature of a process (of a life and a work) that like Dora's analysis was violently broken off. There is a third meaning of anamnesis that I have postponed until now. The anamnesis that is the recollection of things past and the patient's account of her medical history is also "that part of the Eucharistic canon in which the sacrifice of Christ is recalled."[39] García Lorca acolytes as varied as Schonberg, Auclair, and Gibson have each left accounts of their retracing of the road to Víznar in a Calvary that is ever renewed. While I am sympathetic toward the role of repetition in preserving testimony to terror (most particularly in the case of an event without witnesses such as García Lorca's murder), I suggest that it might be truer to the legacy of García Lorca's complex and critical texts to move from the truth of the life to the life of the truth. In other words, rather than impose a fixed meaning on the past, we should attempt (in Foucault's resonant phrase) "an archeology of the present," a process that, like the psychoanalytic case study, will be intelligible only when it has been completed. This need not imply a disavowal of those intense and varied emotions that so many have invested in the figure of the poet; after all, Freud and Breuer warn that, in the clinical context at least, recollection without affect is to no purpose (p. 57). Rather, in analytical two-step with García Lorca, one step behind and facing always back to front, we may finally find a way of remembering toward the future.

4

García Lorca and the Socialists
Subsidized Cinema, Pasqual's Public, and the Identification of Affect

1. Biographism, Familiarity, Fatality

Any scholar approaching the figure of García Lorca in Spain under the Socialist governments of the 1980s will be struck by a number of paradoxes. The first relates to the equivalence of life and work. It is frequently assumed that, on the one hand, biography can explain the true meaning of the text and that, on the other, quotations from that text constitute an authoritative commentary on the life. The second relates to the ubiquity of García Lorca. While representations of the playwright and citations from his work are frequent in cinema and print journalism, it remains the case that in spite of the excellence of individual productions there is no continuous tradition of performance of the plays. Finally, there is the problem of identification and fatality. Central to the cult of García Lorca are the beliefs that the playwright embodies both the particular character of the nation and a universal human condition; and that his death marks him out as a unique individual, a tragic figure whose sacrifice was inevitable and, obscurely, redemptive. These preconceptions interact in curious ways. For example, the stereotype of the tragic destiny of García Lorca was not strong enough to prevent Televisión Española from using the first line of one of García Lorca's *Romancero Gitano* (*Gypsy Ballads*) as the title for its recent gardening program: "Verde, que te quiero verde" ("Green, how I love you, green"). TVE thus assumes the television audience's familiarity with the line, even as it wrenches the quotation out of its poetic context. I return to this poem (the "Romance sonámbulo" or "Sleepwalker's Ballad") in my discussion of an educational film made as an homage to García Lorca and intended for primary-school children.

In this final chapter I hope to exemplify some of the foregoing assumptions (biographical determinism, ubiquity, fatal predestination) by addressing the figure of García Lorca and its reception in three different media – biopics and educational feature films, press reports of cinematic adaptations of the plays, and the commentary of one influential director (Lluís Pasqual) on his own dramatic productions. I refer, incidentally, to a number of plays – to *Bodas de sangre* (*Blood Wedding*) and *La casa de Bernarda Alba* (*The House of Bernarda Alba*); to *El público* (*The Public*) and *Comedia sin título* (*Play Without a Title*) – before focusing in more detail on Pasqual's 1986 production of *El público* for the Centro Dramático Nacional and the Theater of Europe. However, this survey is by no means exhaustive, and the texts themselves are not my main concern. Rather I hope to examine the meanings acquired by the García Lorca cult at a time when the Socialist government was committed to a progressive cultural policy, characterized by such features as tolerance toward minorities, identification with the victims of fascism, and an assertion of cultural continuity before and after the Dictatorship.[1] We shall see that these meanings are often contradictory and perhaps more conflictive than might be supposed.

These contradictions are already clear in an important film of the Transition to democracy, Jaime Chávarri's *A un díos desconocido* (*To an Unknown God*) (1977).[2] The director had recently released another film whose title, *El desencanto* (*The Disenchantment*), clearly expressed its claim to represent the state of the nation at the time in which it was made. The narrative of *A un Díos* has similar aspirations – an older gay man returns in 1974 to the Granada in which García Lorca and his own father had been killed forty years earlier. Obsessed with the poet, the film's hero finally comes to assume his own sexual identity and to reveal to his young lover his intimate identification and secret obsession with García Lorca.

Contemporary press coverage of the film (one of several on a gay theme released at that time)[3] reveals an anxiety over the use of the figure of García Lorca that will recur even ten years later, when democracy was firmly established under the Socialists. One journalist reads the time frame of the somewhat elliptical narrative as a "defense of freedom" that "places historical limits on an individual trauma and the development of internal problems";[4] another stresses more clearly the integration of national and personal narratives in the figure of the poet: "García Lorca . . . is the guiding thread which leads to the protagonist taking on board both the historical past and the immediate present."[5] However, this identification of individual and collective in the text and body of García Lorca is qualified by journalists' persistent nervousness as to the homosexuality of the character in the film and the historical poet – to take one example, the rightist *Ya* cites the film's "prurient allusions" to "personal defects" attributed to García Lorca.[6]

The narrative of *A un díos* depends on the supposed equivalence of life and work in García Lorca (the main character is obsessed both with his memory of the historical poet playing the piano and with the poems that survived him); and it exploits García Lorca's sacrificial death as a metaphor for the quiet fatality of the protagonist's wasted and repressed inner life. But the reception of the film reveals that this movement from personal to national (so characteristic of later representations of the playwright) will be called into question by the homosexuality that Chávarri is the first in Spain to render explicitly and sympathetically. Moreover, in its sacralization of a Granada frozen fetishistically in the memory of the protagonist, it reveals a failure to address the specifically regional nature of García Lorca's achievement, a failure that will also be echoed in the decade that followed.

2. *Representing the Life:* Lorca, muerte de un poeta (Lorca: Death of a Poet) *(1987), and* El balcón abierto *(The Open Balcony) (1984)*

In this section I address two feature films, made with the assistance of the Ministry of Culture and Spanish state television in the mid-1980s. J. A. Bardem's *Lorca, muerte de un poeta* is based on the historical works of Ian Gibson, who had recently produced an exhaustive biography of the dramatist.[7] Jaime Camino's *El balcón abierto* provides useful insight into the values conventionally ascribed to

García Lorca and his work as they were presented to schoolchildren – the film, a poetic collage of scenes from García Lorca's theater and visual interpretations of his poems, is framed by scenes
shot at an authentic primary school in Madrid in which the young
pupils are preparing an "homage" to García Lorca.[8] As we shall
see, in spite of the formal differences between the works (with Bardem's earnest literalism contrasting with Camino's metaphorical
lyricism), they share characteristics that may be attributed to a certain Socialist cultural ethos. Moreover, both films begin and end
with reconstructions of García Lorca's death, thus reinforcing the
commonplace that it is in that fatal moment that life and work find
their fulfillment.[9]

Lorca, muerte de un poeta begins (after the pre-credit death
sequence to which I return in a moment) with an aerial shot of the
arid Castilian meseta. Titles announce the time and place (Spain
1936), and a disembodied voiceover informs us that "These fields
will soon be full of corpses." The next sequence shows us García
Lorca, played by the dubbed British actor Nicholas Grace, reading
the last lines of Bernarda Alba ("Silence. Silence I said") to an ador-
ing audience of fellow poets at a private house in Madrid. The prediction motif returns, this time in the dialogue: "Something terrible is about to happen." The third sequence shows García Lorca
and Rafael Martínez Nadal alone at an outdoor bar outside Madrid – the latter tells us that with the assassination of Fascist Calvo
Sotelo, the "curtain has risen on the first act of the Spanish tragedy."
After these opening sequences, the rest of Lorca, muerte de un poeta
takes place in Granada. But it has already been established that García Lorca's death will be (like the Civil War itself) a kind of fatal
necessity, impossible to avoid, and predestined by García Lorca's
most intimate friends, by his glittering social milieu, and by the very
land itself, the once-fertile plains that now require the redemptive
flow of blood sacrifice.

Yet, in spite of this mythmaking, Bardem's dogged direction
meticulously attempts to re-create historical reality, hour by hour
and street by street. Titles inform us of the exact time at which

events took place, and those events are re-created in the very sites at which they originally occurred. The cult of García Lorca is thus served through adherence to the criterion of cinematic "authenticity," of the equivalence of past action and present reenactment. Moreover, cinematic technique works, discreetly, to place a political interpretation on events presented without explicit commentary – thus the sound of the choir singing at a Mass attended by the Nationalist insurgents is carried over in an ironic sound bridge to the next sequence in which Loyalists are taken in trucks to their place of execution. Implicit political commentary is also built into the casting; for example, Ruiz Alonso (generally held responsible for García Lorca's death) is played by Angel de Andrés López, an actor known for such roles of brutal insensitivity as the husband in Almodóvar's ¿ Qué he hecho yo para merecer esto? (What Have I Done to Deserve This?) (1984).

More characteristic of the film as a whole, however, is the alternation between groups shots of rapid movement (such as street fighting and executions) and slow zooms or pans leading us toward an isolated García Lorca – at his parents' house outside the city, at his hideout inside it, in his prison cell, and finally in the building to which he was confined before the shooting. In spite of the meticulous historicity of Lorca, muerte de un poeta, then (with all principal figures and events clearly and dispassionately identified), the cinematographic style produces a somewhat different effect by which the collective, national struggle is separated from the individual, even personal, narrative of a tragic playwright: Bardem cuts from an extreme closeup of García Lorca, sleepless and haunted in bed, to a shot of a bull entering the ring. Or again, gunshots are heard over repeated shots of the ominously lowering moon. Motifs drawn from García Lorca's work and from a national iconography thus serve to ratify, even legitimize, his death, lending it an inevitability and lyricism wholly abstracted from the brutally chaotic and almost banal story recounted by the rest of the film.

These twin themes of lyricism and fatality also underpin Camino's El balcón abierto. As the pupils pin up photos of García

Lorca in the opening sequence (including a picture of Víznar, the place of his death), they speculate as to the cause of the playwright's murder. And as the film continues, a number of techniques serve, as in *Lorca, muerte de un poeta*, to abstract the narrative of García Lorca's life and to disqualify social or historical interpretations of his work. The first is the use of the same actors to play figures in the poet's life and as characters drawn from the full range of his theatrical and poetic works. Thus the sullen young man known as El Amargo ("The Bitter Man," played by Antonio Flores) appears first as a "giant youth" who spies on the child Federico through the open balcony of the title and recurs as one of the pair of *compadres* in the enigmatic "Romance sonámbulo" and as the *novia*'s lover in a brief extract from *Bodas de sangre*. Or again Amparo Muñoz is at once a mysterious young woman glimpsed by El Amargo at the Sevillian Easter procession (unrelated to any García Lorca text); the "niña amarga" ("bitter girl") sought by the *compadre* in "Romance sonámbulo"; and the Adela of *Bernarda Alba*, confessing her love before she commits suicide. The two actors thus embody the quintessential male and female partners of a heterosexual romance that is held to transcend the banal limits of time and space. Indeed, in spite of their repeated association with Andalusian folkloric motifs (the Easter *pasos* and processions, the flamenco *tablao*, the Alhambra and white houses of the sierra), the recurrence of the actors comes to signify a progressive politics in which sympathy is directed toward sacrificial victims of oppression of whatever place or time.

The sequence intended to illustrate *Poeta en Nueva York* (*Poet in New York*) is exemplary here. Familiar shots of Sixth Avenue glass and steel skyscrapers or the World Trade Center (unbuilt, of course, in García Lorca's time) are shown with a voiceover of the poet denouncing the empty materialism of the City. Voyeuristic and willfully pathetic documentary shots of burnt-out buildings and street people in Harlem are run with a soundtrack of plangent *cante jondo*. The specific history of African Americans (the acknowledgment that the Harlem of the 1920s was not the same as the Harlem of the 1980s) is thus abstracted into a universal victimhood in which blacks are indistinguishable from the Andalusian gypsies of García Lorca's ballads: Camino even has a white horse pace about beneath the detritus of the Brooklyn Bridge, a visual rhyme for the Arab stallions he had already placed in the hills overlooking Granada.

But if regionalism is problematic in *El balcón abierto*, at once reified as folklore and displaced into facile multiculturalism, then homosexuality is yet more difficult to address. For example, in one moment of the frame narrative (the schoolchildren's preparation of the homage to García Lorca) we find two pupils discussing the playwright – one insists he had a boyfriend, not a girlfriend; the other asks, somewhat stiffly, "Was he homosexual?" It is a question that *El balcón abierto* raises but pointedly refuses to answer. In the New York sequence once more we see a trio of bare-chested men (two black, one white) embrace silently, to the sound of a gospel singer repeating the word "Freedom." This sequence not only collapses black and gay liberation, suggesting somewhat problematically that the struggle for the two "freedoms" is one and the same; it also provides an "alibi" (etymologically, "another place") for García Lorca's homosexuality as it was expressed in the context of the Spain of the 1920s and 1930s. Contemporary New York stands in for the schoolchildren's own immediate country, and the love of one Spaniard for another (of, say, García Lorca for Rafael Rodríguez Rapún) is displaced onto foreign bodies – black and white, but clearly not Hispanic. The laudable liberalism of the Socialist ethos, the will to identify with victim groups and denounce their oppression, thus translates into an indifference to the particular circumstances of García Lorca's life, work, and death and their continuing implications for contemporary Spain.

We come now to the death scenes that, as I mentioned before, open and close both films, suspending the historical life in an instant of resonant and reverent fetishization. In *Lorca, muerte de un poeta* what is most striking is the iconographical references to the Passion of Christ. Dazzling in a white suit, which stands out against his seedy surroundings, the poet's meekness contrasting with the coarseness of the soldiers who escort him to the place of execution,

Figure 4. Nicholas Grace (García Lorca, *center*) retracing Calvary in *Lorca, muerte de un poeta* (*Lorca, Death of a Poet*), J. A. Bardem 1987.

García Lorca walks his last steps flanked by two fellow victims of Fascist persecution – a triangular composition reminiscent of Christ framed by the two thieves (Figure 4). The frame freezes as the guns flash and we begin to hear the last lines of *Bernarda Alba*, which will be read by García Lorca after the credits. Sacrifice (of Christ, of García Lorca, of Adela, or of the *niña* of "Romancero sonámbulo") is thus implicitly consecrated by redemption, and the last words of the poet's last play sacralize his murder, presenting it as a willful, even deliberate gesture on the playwright's part in the face of intolerable repression, rather than an act of political violence inflicted on a powerless victim.

Curiously, perhaps, *El balcón abierto*'s treatment of the death scene is less elegiac, more effective. Unlike in *Lorca, muerte de un poeta* García Lorca himself does not appear. Rather the spectator is made to take up his position – the whole sequence is shot with a handheld subjective camera. Thus we (the camera) are hustled from our cell, down corridors and a staircase at which officials and soldiers continue their daily tasks – eating, typing, arguing. Bundled into a car and pulled out by an abusive official who sneers "Maricón" ("Queer"), we are pushed into the shadows of a dark and indistinct landscape and the camera trembles and falls to the ground as the guns fire.

Initially, perhaps, an overexplicit, even coercive attempt to ensure that a juvenile audience identifies with a writer who died fifty years earlier, this subjective color sequence is intercut with brief closeups of the historical García Lorca, in grainy black and white. In general, *El balcón abierto*'s persistent juxtaposition of disconnected images (an attempt to reproduce the poetic structure of García Lorca's lyric and verse drama) tends, like *Lorca, muerte de un poeta*'s mix of literalism and symbolism, to erase the historical specificity of both work and life. Here, however, the shock of the analytical editing at once re-creates the immediacy of the original experience (first person, color) and frames that experience historically (third person, black and white), making the spectator aware of the particular circumstances and unique significance of an event and a life, beyond facile lyricism and retrospective identification. Moreover, unlike *Lorca, muerte de un poeta*, in which García Lorca and his family speak in wholly Castilian tones, in *El balcón abierto* the voiceover narration is read with a definite, if not pronounced, Andalusian accent. As we shall see, the press responses to cinematic adaptations will call attention to continuing tensions around the integrity of the nation-state and the challenge of regionalism, tensions that are only intermittently erased by *Lorca, muerte de un poeta*'s smoothly mythifying production values or *El balcón abierto*'s earnest liberal moralizing.

3. Adapting the work: Bodas de sangre *and* Bernarda Alba

The main criterion cited by Spanish critics of film versions of García Lorca's dramas in the 1980s is fidelity. However, this appeal to cultural continuity is complicated by a lack of agreement as to the nature of García Lorca's achievement and the significance of his legacy to contemporary Spain. Carlos Saura's *Bodas de sangre* (1981) is a film version of a flamenco ballet devised and danced by Antonio Gades and his company, supplemented by dressing room and rehearsal scenes and by autobiographical sequences from the life of Gades himself.[10] Although it is highly self-conscious and formally distant from García Lorca's original text (the mute dance supplemented intermittently by popular song), still critics agreed that "the most notable thing of all [about the film] is that, in spite of so much reworking, Lorca is by no means travestied, but is rather faithfully understood and expressed."[11] Initially, also, there is some agreement as to the nature of the work to which Saura and Gades have shown such fidelity – the film shows us "the magic of performance," a "depth of emotion, [which is] the same as Lorca's tragedy," "a scent of ritual and barbarism" (A.P.G.). This emotionalism, common to play and film, achieves a kind of representational tabula rasa – using elemental myth to "strip bare" the action[12] and returning cinema to its primal essence: silent film.[13] Although critics insist that the "story of *Bodas de sangre* is known to all,"[14] they find "all of the dramatic content of Lorca's poem" expressed in the dancer's body with its "effort, sweat, weariness, and halting breath."[15] It is a kind of vitalism or immediacy in which a "miracle" has occurred: "Lorca lives" (Maso).[16]

The cultural and commercial context of this artistic phenomenon is, however, more complex than might appear at first sight. And a piece run in the conservative *ABC* reveals the political purposes to which García Lorca and Gades were put.[17] Three years after the film's theatrical release Saura presented it at the first Festival of European Cinema, held in Munich. Praising the recent "Miró law," which had established generous subsidies for "quality" Spanish filmmaking,[18] Saura is reported as speaking in defense of European cinema and stating that "each country has traditions and cultures which must not be forgotten." Saura also stresses the interdependence of European markets (with no single country being large enough to support its own industry) and the importance of television to the development of cinema. His views are echoed by Peter Fleischmann, then chairman of the European

Federation of Directors, who argues for resistance to U.S. cultural penetration and the standardization of European tastes and viewing habits – the latter should not respond to Hollywood's fast food with "Euro-burgers."

It is clear, then, that in spite of Spanish critics' belief in the ingenuous vitalism and poetic mystery of García Lorca's (and Saura's) *Bodas de sangre*, as an example of "quality" Spanish filmmaking, the project must be seen in the context of two commercial criteria – the first is the demand for product from the new European commercial TV channels (specifically mentioned by Fleischmann); the second, the desire to produce films that were both different in kind from increasingly dominant U.S. movies and specifically related to the taste of individual European nations. *Bodas de sangre* thus both represented Spain to itself (its very muteness asserting cultural continuity and repressing discontinuities such as regional accents and histories), and re-presented an already familiar folkloric Spain to its European neighbors, who embraced it enthusiastically – *Bodas de sangre* was shown as part of the first night's programming of Britain's Channel 4, one of the new commercial TV channels that Fleischmann had targeted as vehicles for authentically European fare.

This tension between nationalist abstraction and commercial pragmatism is also apparent in Spanish press coverage of Mario Camus's reverent adaptation of *Bernarda Alba* (1987), an adaptation that I have studied in detail elsewhere.[19] Subsidized both by State television (TVE) and the Ministry of Culture, the film received a mixed reception. The rightist *Ya* begins by noting Camus's impeccable reputation as a director of literary adaptations.[20] Here, the critic claims, Camus has opened up the action, "showing in a very physical fashion, women's way of life: their labor in the kitchen, the laundry, and in embroidery" and thus rendering the dramatic spaces in which the action unfolds "believable." However, this concretization of space and action is intended, modestly, to "illustrate" a text that is now wholly abstract – dwelling in the "Olympian" space of masterpieces, "as alive today as when it was first performed in public." The nation may have changed, but *Bernarda Alba*'s "shadow" has not entirely disappeared. Play and film are thus "an image of the eternal Spain."

El Periódico of Barcelona agrees – the play is "a text which is now and ever will be" a masterpiece.[21] The theme of rural virginity is still "very much our own" and the characters still "recognizable" in a Spain which has "not yet disappeared." However, this Spanish critic is very much aware of foreign productions of the text from the United Kingdom to Hungary, which prove the "greatness" of García Lorca by remaining "faithful" to him in their very different ways. And while exhibiting national pride in a "universal" work, critics also reveal an awareness of the material conditions under which that work survives. Thus a local paper from Oviedo claims both that the play is a "timeless metaphor of eternal Spain" and that its action is determined by the "restricted space of the theatrical stage," which inevitably resists cinematic adaptation.[22] Another critic is more forthright, accusing Camus of bowing to the priorities of Socialist cultural policy, which favors "impeccably produced literary adaptations which aim more to fill the State television's screen quotas than to attract the general audience who attend cinemas."[23] The academicism of *Bernarda Alba* (its muted performances and tasteful art design) make it "most worthy of ministerial subsidies . . . a triumph of good taste . . . over passion, boldness, and creative imagination."

Ironically, then, that authenticating emotion assumed to be characteristic of García Lorca is attributed to *Bodas de sangre* but not to *Bernarda Alba;* the dance drama that dispenses with García Lorca's text is held to be more "faithful" than the adaptation that so faithfully preserves it in aspic. Yet even a production as bland as *Bernarda Alba* raised conflicts at the time of filming. Camus reported that he was denied permission to film the opening scene of the funeral of Bernarda's husband in a church in the province of Seville, with the bishop claiming that the (unspecified) reasons for the denial were "obvious." And if García Lorca's name was still enough to render location filming difficult in Andalusia, then another commercial constraint to the adaptation of his plays emerged – *El Periódico* reported that the playwright's inheritors had received 12 million *pesetas* for the cinematic rights to the play (some $120,000), six or seven times sums previously paid to distinguished living writers for adaptation rights.[24]

The distinguished critic José Luis Guarner put the problem into perspective.[25] Why, he asked, had there been so many adaptations of literary works by the minor Garcías (García Alvarez, Blázquez, Hortelano, and Serrano) and so few made of those of García Lorca? The answer lies both in the hostility to García Lorca of the former Francoist regime and in the persistent fear of Spanish directors intimidated by the dramatist's lyrical language. Guarner cites adaptations from Morocco to Italy that preceded the only Spanish attempts – Saura's *Bodas de sangre* and Camino's *El balcón abierto* (which he cites mistakenly, but significantly, as *El balcón vacío* [*The Empty Balcony*]). While Buñuel had been slated for many years to direct *Bernarda Alba*, it fell to the less ambitious Camus to do so – the theatrical curtain he shows before and after the action reveals that his aim is simply to "illustrate" the theatrical text and to reject "folklore" in favor of an "austere severity": there is no music and only the most muted of *mise-en-scènes*. The aestheticism, professionalism, and frigidity of the film thus qualify it as a prime example of the category "quality cinema" – it is to be watched with respect and "just a little boredom," as is proper for a classic.

One feature of the film unmentioned by any critic is that, in spite of the care taken to shoot in an authentic location, none of the actors attempts an Andalusian accent. And it seems likely that the universalism inherent in the term "quality cinema" (a universalism, which, as we have seen, does not prevent it from representing the nation-state to itself and to other nation-states) cannot tolerate any acknowledgment of regional identity that is not frozen into the folkloric fetish of *Bodas de sangre*. And while academic criticism has sometimes read the play as an allegory of homosexual love (and theatrical productions have cast a male actor as Bernarda), any hint of sexual "diversity" beyond the "very Spanish" theme of rural virginity cannot be allowed to appear. If we look at the writings of García Lorca's most prominent theatrical director, however, we see a subtle and complex awareness of both nationalism and homosexuality that goes far beyond either the ingenuous physical vitalism or the punctilious textual fidelity of his principal cinematic adaptors.

4. Identification and Transformation: Lluís Pasqual

Lluís Pasqual is the most important contemporary director of García Lorca's theater, and his career clearly embodies the tensions (and the opportunities) of both microregionalism (the *autonomías*) and macroregionalism (the European Union). Moving from the Teatre Lliure of Barcelona to the Centro Dramático Nacional of Madrid, and then back once more to Barcelona, Pasqual has both created his work within institutions and commented on the limitations of those same institutions. Thus an interview in *ABC*[26] stresses the constraints of both settings – Pasqual claims that it is impossible to remain for a lengthy period in the capital "unless the structure [of the Centro] changes," dependent as it is on a "political conception" of the role of a national theater; but even the Catalan "Free Theater" is not without limits: Pasqual and his colleagues have refused pressure to transform it into a Catalan Dramatic Center; but the price of their freedom to program freely ("as if [the theater] were a restaurant, where you can do what you want and people can come or not as they please") is economic insecurity: still they require public subsidy for such work.

But if Pasqual rejects the burden of representing either the Spanish state or the Catalan autonomous area, his work is nonetheless inevitably read within those intersecting contexts. *ABC*'s Barcelona edition reported his triumphant production of *El público* (along with fellow Catalan Adolfo Marsillach's staging of Lope's *Antes que todo es mi dama*) under the rubric "Catalunya in Madrid"[27] – it is Catalan "intelligence and timely direction" that has brought the last work of a "universal Grenadine" to the Madrid stage. Inversely, the premiere of Pasqual's equally triumphant production of *Comedia sin título* at the national María Guerrero Theater in Madrid is presented by the press in that city as "the greatest success of Madrid theater" that season, attended by sometime architects of the cultural policy of the national government (Jorge Semprún, Pilar Miró), and by guests who authorize the authenticity of the production (the poet Rafael Alberti, García Lorca's sister Isabel).[28]

But the Centro Dramático Nacional's collaboration with designated "European Theaters" in Italy and France also gave the opportunity for Spaniards to read Pasqual's productions in an international context. Thus on the world premiere of *El público* at Giorgio Strehler's Piccolo Theater in Milan *ABC* gave lengthy coverage of the Italian press's response to the work, focusing on *Corriere della Sera*'s "seven columns" of favorable review and Strehler's promise that the María Guerrero would be upgraded to the status of "European Theater."[29] Or again, the appearance of Pasqual's production at the Odéon in Paris gave rise to comparisons with Franco-Argentine Jorge Lavelli's French-language staging at La Colline.[30] The journalist contrasts differing approaches to this "masterpiece of universal theater" – while Lavelli uses stagecraft to threaten the audience, challenges them directly with "obscenity," and re-creates the scene of the poet's crucifixion with extreme cruelty, Pasqual's production is (he claims) more aestheticist, less confrontational, staging the final sacrifice with more beauty than violence.

But if there is clearly national pride in seeing a Spanish masterpiece produced in foreign centers of theatrical excellence, a pride which can proclaim both that García Lorca is universal and that he is subject to multiple interpretations, then there is continuing unease about the explicitly homosexual theme of *El público*. Pistolesi ends by citing *Corriere* on García Lorca's (unspecified) "erotic diversity"; Quiñonero notes Lavelli's "manifest" and "libertarian" obscenity but chooses not to be more precise. For a conservative daily, then, the cultural prestige acquired abroad by the performance of a still-troubling Spanish work is offset by its continuing "diversity" or "obscenity." It is perhaps no accident that on the day

Pasqual's *El público* premiered in Paris *ABC* should also carry a report praising the "reinvention of flamenco" by young Andalusian performers in the French capital;[31] and that on the day of the world premiere of *El público* in Milan, it carried a brief item claiming that onstage nudity in an unrelated production had caused controversy in Turin.[32] While the marketing of Spanish cultural heritage abroad was to be encouraged (even in its most novel forms), the limits of decency in the theater still required rigorous policing, both at home and elsewhere.

I shall argue that in his own Catalan writings Pasqual displays an intelligent and pragmatic approach to both nationalism and sexuality. But at first sight he seems simply to reconfirm the commonplaces of the García Lorca cult I outlined in the introduction to this chapter.[33] For example, Pasqual claims to feel a special "closeness" to García Lorca, perhaps based on the fact that his own mother was Andalusian (p. 76). Feeling that he had always known García Lorca, he was not surprised to discover when he first read him that the plays were just as he had imagined (p. 77). Pasqual's understanding of the playwright is thus not intellectual but physical. Sharing as they do the same birthdate, Pasqual sees his role as director of García Lorca as simply re-creating the emotion felt by the author at the moment of writing. This fantastic identification (compared by Pasqual to the "transmigration of souls") is consecrated by García Lorca's sister, who (Pasqual relates) told Pasqual she "saw" García Lorca in him when she witnessed his productions (p. 78). His is an intimate love for the playwright, of which he can hardly bring himself to speak. Or again, the role of the director is to "draw blood" from the text (p. 83), to struggle against superficiality (p. 85), just as García Lorca knew that facile commercial success could not make up for the truth of personal failure. García Lorca was thus the victim of a "deterministic" fatality; and just as the playwright showed an intense theatrical commitment, which was not, however, political, so the director must muster the same level of commitment (p. 87). The union of playwright and director thus implies that theater has no past or future (no memory), but only a present (p. 91) – the ideal audience is "virgin" (p. 98)

and has no experience of the "theaterly" theater Pasqual despises
(p. 100).

Pasqual's García Lorca thus exhibits that biographical determinism, reassuring familiarity, and fatal predestination that is the
common currency of popular accounts of García Lorca – life and
work are united in an experience that is always already known and
that is rendered complete by the inevitable but redemptive sacrifice of an early death. Yet there is in Pasqual an opposing movement that lends strength to his productions and tends away from
abstraction and universalism toward materialism and concrete
specificity. Thus there is no doubt that Pasqual has performed a
scholarly, even archaeological, service in staging for the first time
previously unperformed and often unfeasibly short plays (p. 76).
It is not surprising to hear him stress that direction requires a technical apprenticeship, like any other profession (p. 77). And if he
compares himself to García Lorca, he also claims that both of them
love to lie (p. 81). Indeed, lying (rather than any metaphysical
notion of truth or authenticity) is for Pasqual at the heart of García Lorca's achievement and of theater in general. Pasqual laughs
when he calls to mind the difference between *Poeta en Nueva York*
and the letters García Lorca wrote to his family at the same time;
this "splitting of the self" seems "horrific and extraordinary" today;
but it is one that, with his sane laughter (of distance and of recognition), Pasqual can appreciate and understand as the foundation,
also, of the social convention (the lie) that is theater. It thus follows
that in theater, the actor's communication of emotion to the audience is dependent on skill, not the experience of authentic feeling – the boundary between true and false cannot be located (p.
82). In a similar way, the expression of true love in García Lorca (as
in the dialogue of the Figure of Vine Leaves and Figure of Bells in
El público) is always qualified by a "sarcastic voice," deflating meta-
physics and revealing that "humor is the height of intelligence" (p.
84). Hence, if García Lorca was not overtly political, still he sought
to "provoke"; and if theater has no memory, still it may have a
"scent" or "flavor," which Pasqual identifies with a "subterranean"
resistance (p. 90). In this context Pasqual presents his project,

quite explicitly, as a challenge to the hegemony of a complacent Socialist government that has restored the parameters of "normality" supported by politicians of other parties (p. 91). The timid, aestheticist theater that has been achieved under such a regime is not enough – faced with the "pretty things" it has done, Pasqual believes it is necessary to put everything into question once more, to begin again.

Pasqual claims that he seeks not success but recognition – the recognition through which something is explained to the audience that it may not have expected to hear (p. 102). I suggest that it is just this recognition that provokes Pasqual to intelligent laughter when he thinks of García Lorca in New York and that we should use to displace the facile and often maudlin identification so typical of the García Lorca cult. For where phantasmatic identification presupposes a simple equation of playwright and audience (or director) in which the latter, narcissistically, finds what is already known reflected back to him, Pasqual's disabused and sometimes ironic recognition admits of both similarity and difference in a double act of empathy with the same and respect for the other, which permits both intimacy and historical distance. In Pasqual's writings, then, as in his productions, we find both a skeptical awareness of the role played by theater in the national and regional cultural politics of the Spanish state and an attitude of ironic complicity toward the homosexuality of the most prestigious representative of that culture. It is a sophisticated and productive position that in a different medium the more reverent filmmakers, who sought oh-so-seriously to represent García Lorca's life and works, are quite unable to achieve.

We come now to an analysis of Pasqual's highly successful production of *El público* for the Spanish Centro Dramático Nacional and the international Theater of Europe. There are three initial paradoxes about this production. First, what is notoriously the most hermetic and allusive of García Lorca's plays here produces what is by all accounts an unambiguously emotional effect in audiences.[34] Second, the conceptual complexity of the piece is pre-

sented in a simple, stripped-down staging that nonetheless suc-
ceeds in communicating the full complexity of García Lorca's
ideas on both homosexuality and theater. Finally, this example of
"director's theater" (in which the production was sold as much on
Pasqual's name as on García Lorca's)[35] manifests a rigorous respect for the fragmentary text – little is omitted, nothing is
changed, and, as we shall see, the most significant (if enigmatic
lines) are delivered by the actors with clarity and at an appropriate
pace. It is characteristic of the production that the entire script of
the play (little known at the time) was reproduced in the lavish
program, with its graphic design by the respected experimental
artist Frederic Amat and impressionistically blurred production
photographs by Ros Ribas. Although my purpose in this chapter is
not, then, to address primarily the text but rather those resources
specific to performance (such as production design, acting style,
and lighting), aspects of the staging are almost invariably motivated by the text, whether by García Lorca's sporadic stage directions or the dialogue itself. The dividing line between text and production is thus exceedingly difficult to draw.

The simplicity of the design is shown by the single performance
space – a horseshoe-shaped arena constructed by removing the
seats from the stalls and seating the audience in the remaining rows
on three sides of the action. Fabià Puigserver,[36] the production
designer, fills this arena with vivid blue sand terminated only by a
rich, red curtain in front of the original proscenium stage. The
actors enter from opposing ends of the elongated performing
space – either from the door through which the audience itself
entered the theater or from between or under the curtain facing
that entrance. The performance space is thus both ambiguous and
flexible. Abolishing the boundaries between audience and actors
and between front and back of stage, it also lends itself to confrontation – between actors and audience (Julieta and the Silly
Shepherd ["el Pastor Bobo"] address the audience directly) and
between actors (the Director and the three Men or the Director and
the Magician face one another at opposite ends of the arena) (Figure 5). In spite of the exceptionally large cast of some thirty actors,

Figure 5. Lluís Pasqual's *El público* (*The Public*), Madrid 1989. The three Men confront the Director (Alfredo Alcón).

which is of course financially feasible only in a publicly subsidized theater, Pasqual's production is thus economic in both the common and the psychoanalytic senses of the term – it both strips down the acting space to the essentials and carefully martials the quantity of resources available to produce a finely modulated quality of experience. This economic relation between quantity and quality is also the relation between instinct and affect in Freud's "economics" of the psyche.[37] Moreover, as we shall see, the staging (and most particularly the costume and lighting design) lend themselves to the acting out of two complex areas in Freud, to which García Lorca's text also addresses itself in typically allusive and elusive style – the relationship between homosexuality and sociality in group identification and the relationship between the lost object and subjectivity in the ego's identification with the other.

Initially, however, it is clear that Pasqual's *El público* relates back to debates on cultural policy under the Socialists that I have

already addressed in this chapter. The production reveals to mas-
terly effect Pasqual's "archaeological" role in staging a text previously unstaged in Spain. Yet its technical mastery avoids the traps
of academicism, good taste, or "quality"; and in spite of the visual
beauty of the production (most particularly in its bold use of color)
it cannot be accused of aestheticism. Responsive to the text's lack
of geographical precision, the production design is resolutely non-
specific, yet at certain moments that abstraction is undermined by
national touches – a Spanish guitar plays as Juliet returns to the
tomb or a whirling red cape briefly evokes the bullfight. Moreover,
the erotic desire that permeates the text (and whose name even
contemporary Spanish scholars dare not speak)[38] is concretized by
the physicality of performance style in, say, the passionate dance of
power and of pleasure between the two Figures in Cuadro II. If
Pasqual's production remains relatively reticent compared with
Lavelli's in Paris (with less nudity and graphic sexual activity), still
it stages homosexuality without either apology or apologetics. It
thus suggests a new kind of fidelity to the spirit and letter of García
Lorca's text, a fidelity in which homosexuality is neither displaced
onto another scene nor immobilized by an overreverent respect.

To observe this new fidelity in action, let us examine the staging
systematically, comparing it at each point with García Lorca's stage
directions and with pointers in his dialogue. We have seen that
Pasqual's single set replaces García Lorca's multiple sets. It does so,
however, by condensing elements taken from Cuadros I and III.
Thus the "blue scenery" of the opening scene ("decorado azul"; I,
119) is fused with "the wall of sand" in front of which the Director
and Men embrace and struggle ("muro de arena"; III, 141). García Lorca's secondary scenery is consistently cut – the "great hand
printed on the wall" and the X-ray windows ("Una gran mano
impresa en la pared. Las ventanas son radiografías"; I, 119); the
fallen "capital" of the Roman Ruin ("capitel"; II, 131); the "transparent moon" and "great, green leaf shaped like a spearhead"
before the wall of sand ("una luna transparente casi de gelatina,"
"una inmensa hoja verde lanceolada"; III, 141); the "great horse's
head," "enormous eye," and "clump of trees with clouds" ("una

gran cabeza de caballo," "un ojo enorme y un grupo de árboles con nubes"; VI, 181): none of these appear. Out too, go the majority of striking visual effects and idiosyncratic props – the Director's blond wig, which he exchanges for a dark one (I, 121); the Child who falls from the ceiling to announce the Emperor's arrival (II, 136); the opening of the wall to reveal Juliet's tomb and the wheel held by the Black Horse in his hands (III, 146, 151); and the Magician's disappearing trick with the Lady who is mourning her son (VI, 187).

What is striking, however, is the respect with which García Lorca's description of the costumes is reproduced, most particularly in the color scheme of black, white, red, and blue. Thus the Director and three Men wear identical white tie and tails, initially at least (I, 119, 121), until the former is transformed into an actress in white satin holding a tiny black guitar (I, 126) and the Second Man into a woman dressed in a black pajama suit with a garland of poppies (I, 127). White, too, as specified in the text, are Juliet's "opera gown" and the Magician's satin cape, while the Ballerina's costume (unspecified) is white with a red bodice. The White Horses, whose costume is also unspecified, are bare-chested with black boots, white jodhpurs, black muzzles, and long white wigs for manes. Where Puigserver differs from García Lorca, the change of costume serves to supplement a certain reading of the text – thus while the stage directions tell us the two Figures are "totally covered" ("cubierta[s] totalmente"; II, 131) with red vine leaves or little bells, in Pasqual's production these attributes are detachable and may be put on or taken off at will, in accordance with the shifting power play of the dialogue. In another case, the episode of the Emperor's implied murder of the Child, which does not appear in the production, is substituted by the Emperor's burlesque striptease, complete with musical accompaniment. Here the removal of red and black gloves, which is specified in the text, is exaggerated to camp effect. Costume thus substitutes for a scene that has been cut, just as before (in the case of the Figures) costume reinforces the implications of a dialogue that is indeed delivered by the actors.

Acting style is also responsive to, but not determined by, written stage directions. Thus Maruchi León's quicksilver performance as Julieta is suggested by García Lorca's prompts in which the character is alternately "trembling," "furious," and "weeping" ("temblando," "furiosa," "llorando"; III, 148; 149) (Figure 6). Or again the Figures' shifting game of dominance and submission is already sketched by the stage directions in which they speak alternately: "shyly," "forcefully," "stronger," "weaker," "vibrant," "faded," "trembling," "rising," "anguished," "weak-voiced," "falling to the ground," and "approaching in a low voice" ("tímidamente," "enérgico," "más fuerte," "más débil," "vibrante," "desfallecido," "tembloroso," "levantándose," "angustiado," "con voz débil"; II, 132–5) (Figure 7). The hints of movement and body position here are fully developed by Pasqual and his actors in their very physical and erotic version of the scene. Entering the arena from under the curtain in a blackout and to a deafening drumroll, the two Figures are first seen kneeling and facing each other in a brightly illuminated but irregular space defined by lights on the blue sand. Both then sprawl luxuriantly on the ground, before the Figure of Vine Leaves slowly rises, taunting his prone companion for his weakness, and circles him, cracking a whip. The positions are then reversed with the Figure of Bells on top, emphatically voicing his own qualified version of manhood as he circles his crouching partner and even briefly adopting the top position in anal sex, forcing himself between his lover's thighs.[39] In this "economical" scene, the play of intensities of voice and body movement is subtly varied, transforming a fluctuating quantity of instinctual energy into a finely differentiated range of affective qualities.

A similar economy of means and sensitivity to the text is shown by the use of differing registers of acting style. Thus the Director, the Men, and (later) the Red Nude deliver their densely figurative lines urgently or tenderly, as the case may be, but always naturalistically and with due attention to both poetic resonance and conceptual significance. The allegorical costume characters, however, such as the Harlequin and the woman in black pajamas (into

Figure 6. Lluís Pasqual's *El público* (*The Public*), Madrid 1989. Julieta
(Maruchi León) confronts the three White Horses.

whom the Director and Second Man have been transformed),
adopt a highly rhetorical and stylized delivery and a grating,
falsetto tone of voice. The line between subjective and objective
dramatic action, a line that critics have spent much time vainly
attempting to draw, is here reproduced in a manner that is immediately accessible to the audience (no spectator could fail to notice
the difference in performance style), but one that is also fragile
and variable (the White Horses rhythmically chant their lines to
the Director in Act I but solemnly declaim them to Julieta in Act
III). Once more the resources of the production at once comple-
ment and outstrip the text itself.

   But the richest resource of this performative supplement is
lighting design. Lighting is used as a substitute for and an addition
to scenery, effects, and props, which are generally absent in the
production. The most spectacular case of this kind is the circular
screen (*biombo*) behind which the Director and Men pass in
Cuadro I, only to reappear in their stylized feminine costumes.

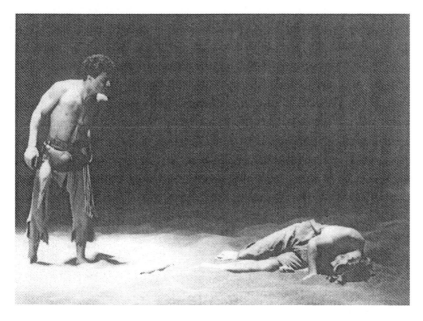

Figure 7. Lluís Pasqual's *El público* (*The Public*). Madrid 1989. The two Figures (Angel Pardo, *left;* Vicente Díez, *right*) struggle.

Here the rather clumsy prop is replaced by the more flexible technique of moving spotlights in a blackout, which shift suddenly from one actor to another. The costumes serve (as is suggested by the text itself and by García Lorca's manuscript revisions)[40] to render more difficult the audience's recognition of the characters – different characters are dressed identically while the same character adopts different disguises. Inversely, however, lighting is used, critically and in ways unspecified by the text, to establish connections and to make distinctions between, and indeed within, characters.

To take an early example: In Cuadro I the director is initially held in a fixed spotlight at one end of the performing space, while the three Men confront him from the shadows at the other end. The First Man then advances to the edge of the Director's light-space and stretches out a hand that the Director does not take. When the Director makes an impassioned speech on the power of social convention (on "the mask"), he leaves the safety of his spot and ventures into the Men's shadow, only to retreat back to it when he is taunted for his mendacity by the First Man. The lighting design and placement of the actors thus renders transparent the opaque dialogue, establishing immediately the Director's separation from, attraction to, and renewed isolation from his former lover, who is dressed identically to him. The most ephemeral or insubstantial theatrical resource, lighting is here also the most immediate in its theatrical effect and in its affective charge. I will suggest a little later how the final Cuadro establishes an unexpected identification between the Director and the First Man, one that is not explicitly motivated by the text. It is a scene in which the Director tells the Magician, with a concision and abstraction typical of García Lorca's dialogue, that substitution is a more difficult job than addition or subtraction (VI, 187). In Pasqual's *El público*, lighting design serves as just such a substitution, neither giving nor taking away but rather transforming the dead letter of the text by suffusing it with a luminous illusion of life.

Lighting thus serves on the one hand to create a flexible and provisional acting space (from the limits of the Director's circular spotlight to the expanses of the Figures' less circumscribed area); but on the other hand it serves to delineate character, defining the spaces between and within them. It is in this context that aspects of Freud's later accounts of the social and the subjective (of identification and of affect) become cogent. Thus in "Some Neurotic Mechanisms in Jealousy, Paranoia, and Homosexuality" (an essay first published in 1922 to which I have already referred), Freud gives two conflicting accounts of the etiology of male homosexuality.[41] The first is based on identification with the mother – attachment to this first, feminine love object is combined with narcissism (the choice of an object who possesses a penis like oneself) and fear of castration (the retreat from rivalry with the father) (p. 206). The second (Freud's "new mechanism") is based on identification among members of a group – in this case jealous impulses toward male rivals for the mother's affection "yielded to repression and underwent a transformation, so that the rivals of the earlier period became the first homosexual love objects" (p. 207). In this second model (unlike in the first) "homosexual attitudes . . . did not exclude heterosexuality and did not involve a *horror feminae*" (p. 207).

Freud finds, however, that this model of homosexual object choice as a "reactive formation against repressed aggressive impulses" (p. 207) is difficult to square with his theory of sublimated homosexuality as the basis for sociality among (self-consciously) heterosexual men. On the one hand, homosexuals may have well-developed social instincts because they view "other men as potential love objects [not] jealous rivals" and because they have overcome rivalry with men (p. 208). On the other hand, Freud is aware that jealousy and rivalry are not unknown even among homosexuals, who have supposedly repressed such unsocial instincts. Dismissing this empirical evidence as a "speculative explanation," Freud concludes that in homosexuals "the detachment of social feeling from object choice is not fully carried out," as it is in the case of heterosexual men, whose jealous and rivalrous love of women can be socialized only by sublimated homosexual feelings for their fellows.

Now both of Freud's models of homosexual etiology are acted out in the text of *El público*. A feminine, regressive, and narcissistic object choice is seen in the transformations of the Director and Men into stylized women in silk pajamas or ballerina costumes. I argue, however, that these male metamorphoses should be read not (as they frequently have been) as the revelation of a true or authentic self but rather as identifications in what Lacan calls the "full" sense of the term – the transformation of the subject when he or she assumes an image.[42] For if the mirror play of the identically dressed Men and Horses (who are identified with each other in the text and manuscript) suggests narcissism and regression, García Lorca is concerned above all with the interpenetration of subjectivity and sociality. As a play explicitly concerned with the twin themes of love and theater, *El público* dramatizes identification among the members of a group (of lovers, of actors, and of spectators), an identification in which two or more partners are mutually transformed. Thus in the repeated struggles and embraces of the two Figures, of the Director and the First Man, and of the Second and Third Men, García Lorca suggests that the aggressive instincts of jealousy and rivalry are indeed prototypes of homosexual object choice and are inseparable from sexual desire and genital pleasure.

However, *pace* Freud, in *El público* that jealousy and rivalry are by no means repressed but rather coexist with love. The problem, then, for García Lorca is one not addressed by Freud – the possibility of a sociality between homosexuals, of a group identification whose erotic charge would neither be safely sublimated as it is in heterosexuals, nor psychically or socially repressed as it is in homosexuals subjected as we are to pervasive and invasive homophobia. Taunting one another for their cowardice, glorying in their momentary strength, or lamenting the mask of social convention that "buttons us up in the middle of the street" ("En medio de la calle, la máscara nos abrocha los botones"; III, 156), still *El público*'s men cannot stop being men ("¿Es que un hombre puede dejar de serlo nunca?"; III, 142). It is a masculine identification as violent as any untamed heterosexual relation. But, unlike the latter, it is untainted by misogyny or *horror feminae* – Julieta's response to the White Horses (trembling, furious, weeping) is identical to that of the male characters when they are confronted by the urgent demands of the erotic.

This, then, is one specific contribution of the staging to García Lorca's text. Juliet is caressed by the Horses in Cuadro III, just as the Director had been in Cuadro I; she mounts one of the Horses, as one Figure mounted another in Cuadro II; finally, she returns to her tomb to the sound of the same Spanish guitar that is heard over the Red Nude's death agony. Equating the homosexual man and the heterosexual woman not in respect to a supposed feminine identification but rather in relation to a sociality from which each is in different ways excluded (a sociality based on sublimated erotic relations among heterosexual men), García Lorca and Pasqual suggest the violent and pleasurable (the dramatic) effects of a persistent, necessary, and perhaps impossible attempt to integrate social feeling and object choice, which would no longer remain detached in Freud's prescribed manner.

If sociality is based, problematically and provisionally, on group identification, then subjectivity or affect is based on the ego's identification with the object. Freud's essay "Mourning and Melancholia" of 1917, to which I have also referred earlier,[43] charts a "shattering" of the object-relationship in which libido is "withdrawn into the ego" and "the conflict between the ego and the loved person [transformed] into a cleavage between the critical activity of the ego and the ego as altered by identification" (p. 258). Erotic cathexis is thus subject to a "double vicissitude: part of it has regressed to identification, but the other part, under the influence of the conflict due to ambivalence, has been carried back to the stage of sadism" (p. 261). This for Freud is the solution to the "riddle of the tendency to suicide . . . in melancholia" in which "thoughts of suicide [are] turned back upon [one]self from murderous impulses against others." He concludes: "In the opposed situations of being most intensely in love and of suicide the ego is overwhelmed by the object, though in totally different ways" (p. 261).

I suggest that this transformation of object loss into ego loss (this identification of the ego with the desired and despised loved person) might explain the combination of sadistic and suicidal impulses in the final Cuadros of *El público*. The sadism is seen in the treatment of the Red Nude, suspended on a perpendicular bed (one of the few props Pasqual preserves from García Lorca's text) and attended by a callously indifferent Male Nurse (V, 165) (Figure 8). The text echoes the staging's transparent allusion to the Crucifixion but, like the staging once more, it historicizes, even banalizes, supreme sacrifice. Thus the Nude asks how far it is to Jerusalem and the Nurse replies that that depends on the supplies of coal that are left; the Nude cries out for the cup to be taken away from him and the Nurse castigates him for breaking another thermometer; finally the Nude gives up his spirit to the Lord and the

Figure 8. Lluís Pasqual's *El público* (*The Public*), Madrid 1989. The Red Nude (Juan Matute), crucified, with the Nurse (Chema de Miguel Bilbao).

Nurse complains that he is running two minutes fast (V, 166; 172). Metaphysical suffering is thus brought down to earth – the Nude laments the agony of man who is alone "on platforms and in trains" ("la agonía del hombre solo, en las plataformas y en los trenes"; V, 172).[44]

The bed then turns on its vertical axis (in both García Lorca and Pasqual) to reveal the First Man, still dressed in his tails, in the position previously occupied by the Nude (Figure 9). His lament, however, is crucially different:

Soledad del hombre en el sueño lleno de ascensores y trenes donde tú vas a velocidades inasibles. Soledad de los edificios, de las esquinas, de las playas, donde tú no aparecerás ya nunca. (V, 176–7)

Solitude of [the] man in a dream of lifts and trains in which *you* travel at ungraspable speeds. Solitude of buildings and corners, of beaches, where *you* will never appear again.

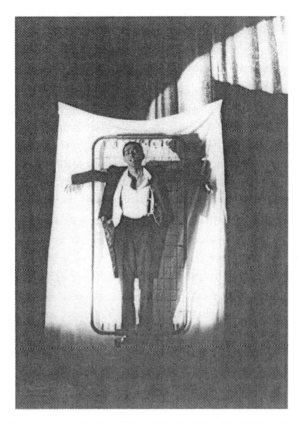

Figure 9. Lluís Pasqual's *El público* (*The Public*), Madrid 1989. The First Man (Joan Miralles), crucified.

The actor Joan Miralles gives his lines a hoarse, urgent pathos. Metaphysical solitude, already historicized, is here addressed to the absent or abandoned other ("tú"), the personal love object whose loss has cast a "shadow"[45] over the ego and caused the subject's dereliction.

In the subsequent, final Cuadro the Director seems unmoved by what has gone before, coldly dismissing the First Man's mother, who in a further echo of the Passion of Christ comes seeking her dead son's body. Yet after his Dialogue with the Magician (who is generally identified by critics as the figure of Fate comparable to the card players at the end of *Así que pasen cinco años*), the Director is reduced to silence, to solitude, and to death – in García Lorca, as again in Pasqual, the play ends in bitter cold and with snow falling.

But here once more and finally, light design supplements a willfully disorientating text to provide a further and conclusive identification – at the start of Cuadro VI the Director is caught in a spotlight in the same position as the Nude and First Man (that is, on the opposite side of the acting space from that on which he had begun Cuadro I and to which he has tended always to return) (Figure 10). When the Director puts himself in the place of his ex-lover (albeit unattached to a bed), his final melancholia is presented as a repressed and ambivalent identification with the loved person; and the ironically distant Magician is transformed into the critical activity of the ego that has been "cleft" and separated from the impoverished ego as altered by identification (the Director, who disappears into the shadow, into the snow). Object loss thus becomes ego loss and sadism suicide. Yet even here, in amorous dereliction and self-absorption, the fragile circle of the spotlight suggests (like Freud's version of mourning and melancholia) the possibility of a continuing relation between subjectivity and sociality even in extremis and the persistent permeability of individual boundaries. It is a fitting, final image of theater (of homosexuality) as an encounter with the other, a work of love in which audience and work are mutually, erotically transformed.

5. From Sacrifice to Memory

We have seen that it is an article of faith of the García Lorca cult not only that life and literature are one, but that death takes precedence over life and defines the final meaning of literature. I suggested in the survey of diverse cinematic and print texts in the first half of this chapter that the very ubiquity of this biographical determinism and fatalism inspired a phantasmatic identification used in quite specific ways in the Spain of the 1980s – Bardem used the death of García Lorca as a replaying of the Crucifixion even as he insisted on the historical re-creation of the Civil War, while Camino

Figure 10. Lluís Pasqual's *El público* (*The Public*), Madrid 1989. The Director caught in the spotlight.

led schoolchildren to associate the playwright with all victims of oppression in all periods, from Granada to Harlem, and from the 1930s to the present day. Cinematic adaptors sought to enlist García Lorca for their own ideals of liberal tolerance on the one hand, or conservative national identity on the other. The successful theatrical productions of Pasqual, like the less well realized cinematic adaptation of Camus, were among the most visible ways in which Spaniards chose to represent cultural continuity to themselves and to others and to repress their true awareness of the national (and indeed the sexual) diversity of their state and its cultural inheritance.

This chapter has been a study not so much of the richness of García Lorca's text but of the diversity of reactions to it. In the rather contradictory manner of Freud's concept of overdetermination[46] we have seen that one figure (such as García Lorca) can be made to bear many different meanings; but also that one meaning (liberal tolerance or redemptive sacrifice) can be expressed by many figures – also pressed into service by socialist cultural policy were other progressive texts of a previous era, which received the same "quality" cinematic treatment as *Bernarda Alba*.[47] I argue, however, that if we abandoned the motif of sacrifice, we might begin to recover a cultural memory that is fully embodied, in the theatrical performer or in the life of the citizen as it is lived in time. It is this coextensiveness of life and work in the memory of the subject (wholly different from the violent collapsing of author's life and work in the García Lorca cult) that was offered to Spaniards at the dawning of democracy in Chávarri's prescient *A un díos desconocido,* to which I referred at the beginning of this chapter.

And if, as I suggest, sacrifice is replaced by memory and phantasmatic identification by identification in its "full" (Lacanian) sense, then this offers a new opportunity for rereading García Lorca's works, an opportunity already and most powerfully suggested by Lluís Pasqual's writings and productions. We can then seek a revised approach to regionalism in García Lorca that would appeal neither to folklore nor to a reified nationalism but rather would address the unstable but fruitful position of an Andalusia caught between a fragile Spanish federal state and the possibility of a European Union of the regions; and it would suggest a new approach to homosexuality in García Lorca that would neither be abstracted into a bland "tolerance" nor reduced to a fixed identity but would rather stand as a privileged instance of that social negotiation between truth and lie that is for Pasqual (and perhaps for García Lorca) the foundation of both theater and civil society. This chapter can only point the way to such readings, just as it has examined only a fraction of the cultural references to García Lorca in the Spain of the 1980s. If we move beyond the confines of the cult, however, we may find that the true success of García Lorca's theater is not confined to that which is already known to us. We may then be led to know things that we were by no means expecting – as members of the audience, as scholars, or as lovers of García Lorca struggling, like the Men and Figures of *El público,* through affect and beyond mourning to a new, fuller sense of identification.

Conclusion
"Doing Lorca"

This book began with the transfer of the Fundación García Lorca to the same site as the Residencia de Estudiantes in Madrid; and with the opening of the Casa-Museo in the Huerta de San Vicente, outside Granada. The latter was presented in the national *El País* as an act of postponed "reconciliation" between the poet and his home town. The true story as told in the regional press was, however, more complex. For García Lorca's archive had originally been offered to Granada council, which had rejected it. When it and the regional government of Andalusia later requested the archive be transferred from Madrid, generously offering the recently opened Huerta de San Vicente as its site and pledging an annual subsidy of five million *pesetas*, the director of the Fundación, Manuel Fernández Montesinos, was said to have refused their offer. The Andalusian *Ideal* reported that the Casa-Museo, in its current, more modest incarnation, had recently been closed because of the town council's delay in paying its employees' wages.[1]

This continuing struggle between center and periphery staged around the figure of García Lorca was also seen at an auction of unpublished manuscripts by the poet. On this occasion the national State exercised its right of first refusal by spending almost five million *pesetas* and thus leaving both the Fundación and the Casa-Museo empty-handed. *ABC* reported that the final destination of the documents would be decided by the then Socialist Minister of Culture, Carmen Alborch.[2] This acquisition was part of Madrid's cultural policy at the time – a substantial portion of Buñuel's papers was also to be bought later for a much larger sum.[3]

Hence García Lorca remained a site of struggle in Spain, as he was abroad. Thus if García Lorca was in the 1990s the foreign playwright most frequently staged in Britain, still references to Brecht far outnumbered those to García Lorca in the British quality press.[4] Even as García Lorca's universal genius is proclaimed, still his influence on theater in general is restricted – the fact that there is no standard adjective in English derived from his name, equivalent to the familiar "Brechtian," confirms that this is the case. Moreover, it is difficult to trace any conceptual or intellectual influence abroad, analogous to that of Brecht once more, that might be attributed to García Lorca's "impossible," experimental works. Presented as ever as a seductive icon rather than a playwright of substance, García Lorca was the subject of yet another biopic – in winter 1995 Marcos Zurinaga began shooting the stereotypically titled *Blood of a Poet*, starring Esai Morales and Andy Garcia. Based on Ian Gibson's books, the film was intended in familiar fashion to focus not on the life or the work of García Lorca but rather on his death.[5]

In Spain, critics continued to complain about García Lorca scholars' supposed "obsession with sex and politics," with one venerable figure from Granada claiming that this tendency had "rendered uncongenial ['antipática'] the figure of Lorca, who was congeniality ['simpatía'] itself, the most vibrant joy and youthfulness of a whole glorious period of our literature."[6] In a hermetic "Spanish literary system"[7] that jealously preserved its immunity from the critical fashions of English-speaking countries, it remained difficult to acknowledge that "congeniality" might be culturally conditioned or dependent on the suppression of those very factors (such as homosexuality) that a national literary tradition would have the most difficulty in assimilating. It is perhaps not in scholarly studies but in Frederic Amat's artistic works, endlessly repeated graphic traces intended for a traveling theater that was never to be built, that we find one of the most touching and challenging responses in the Spanish state to García Lorca's restlessly experimental legacy.[8]

Like French productions of García Lorca in the 1950s and 1960s, Spanish productions in the 1990s oscillated between folklore and abstraction. The most transparent example of the first tendency was Luis Olmos's production of *La zapatera prodigiosa* (*The Shoemaker's Wonderful Wife*) for the Teatro de la Danza de Madrid,[9] which, after completing a national tour, played the capital's Teatro La Latina from September to November 1995. The venue was significant – this was the first time that a García Lorca play had been staged in this "popular theater." The director reported in an interview that his company specialized in "strong doses of music, dance, color, and, of course, theater";[10] while publicity material also stressed "light, color, and fun ['alegría'] with the unmistakable magic of the great Andalusian poet!" While this popularizing approach may well serve as an antidote to the sometimes anesthetic "quality" versions of García Lorca that I documented in my previous chapter (and most certainly achieved a more resounding commercial success), in Olmos's case a short and fragile text was swamped by a lavish and garish staging, in which the actors were poorly integrated with professional dancers, on sabbatical from the Compañía Nacional de Danza and the Ballet Nacional de España.

At the opposite end of the spectrum came Lluís Pasqual's *Haciendo Lorca* for the Centro Dramático Nacional and the Théâtre de l'Europe, which played Madrid's subsidized Teatro María Guerrero in April and May 1996. Originally announced as a radically pruned production of the text of *Bodas de sangre*, *Haciendo Lorca* reduced theatricality to a bare minimum – two actors (Nuria Espert and Alfredo Alcón); a bare black staging against which the actors were slowly transported on cranes; a text composed of fragments of *Bodas*, *Yerma*, *Así que pasen cinco años*, and *El público*. Coldly received in Andalusia,[11] the somewhat reworked piece received an ecstatic welcome in Madrid. As *El País* reported, the sense of a unique occasion derived in part from the fact that this was "the last premiere of the Socialist era" and the last cultural event at which socialite Minister of Culture Alborch would be present.[12]

While audience and press feted Pasqual as Spain's most international director, recently awarded the French Légion d'Honneur, his innovatory *Haciendo Lorca* is to be read in the context of a newly nationalist programming policy for the Centro Dramático Nacional – it had earlier been announced that the Madrid Centro would focus for that season on twentieth-century Spanish plays.[13] Just as the rapturous reception at the María Guerrero had been underwritten by the news (just announced) that the victorious but minority Partido Popular was to form a government with the Catalan regionalists, so the shift from experimental to classical programming was acknowledged by Pasqual himself to be a response to "this time of disappointment and anguish" in which arts professionals awaited with the rest of the nation an as yet untried right-wing government. Pasqual thus feels a need to return to unfinished business with the "all too familiar" García Lorca ("el Lorca de toda la vida"). But he also stresses the contribution of his actors – Espert, who had starred as *Yerma* in Víctor García's famous production, and Alcón, who had played the Director in Pasqual's own *El público*. Pasqual claims they are "the last great masters with a direct line [to the poet], a specific way of doing Lorca. It was now or never." Here we find once more that sense of the fragility and pathos inherent in the theatrical event and in the contribution of actors, who in the course of their careers exhibit to the audience the trace of time in their bodies – few of those present at the premiere of *Haciendo Lorca* could have failed to be aware of the role played by the playwright, by the actors, and by their director in the theater of the transition to democracy and of the subsequent "disillusion" with the Socialist government.

But the intense affects experienced by many in the audience of *Haciendo Lorca* (*El País* speaks of "rejoicing and tears") are not merely generalized emotion; rather they are also part of what Freud called an "economics of pain" – a work of mourning or progressive "detachment from an object [whose] significance is reinforced by a thousand links."[14] The experience of the theater, continually repeated in time and diffused in space, constructed through the accumulation of countless memory traces and affective charges, seems to be exemplary of just such an economic process. It is a process in which a figure such as García Lorca is gradually endowed with an affective charge and significance whose limits cannot simply be defined.

Freud writes in his case study of female homosexuality that one way of breaking off a love relation is through identification of the lover with the object.[15] I have argued that, merging with their fan-

tasies of García Lorca, many critics and spectators regress to a nostalgic narcissism in which their very own poet (whether sacrificial
blood victim or congenial genius of "our literature") reflects back
to them what they already know. There are recent signs in Spain,
however, that mourning may be coming to an end; and that with
the consequent liberation of affect García Lorca is being incorporated into new and exciting contexts that could not previously have
been anticipated. One of these signs is Pasqual's *Haciendo Lorca*
itself, with its radical disrespect for the integrity of García Lorca's
text. Another is Joaquín Cortés's dance version of "El diálogo del
amargo" ("The Dialogue of the Bitter One"), which formed part of
his highly successful flamenco fusion dance show *Pasión gitana*
(*Gypsy Passion*), first performed in March 1995.[16] Staged as an
amorous *pas-de-deux* between two male dancers, and with García
Lorca's poetry recited over the dance, this is one of the first examples of a Spanish "queering" of García Lorca. The Cortés who rev-
els in his Cordovan heritage but acts for Almodóvar and models for
Armani, the Cortés who displays a muscular male torso while danc-
ing in a skirt, is a fine example of a cultural phenomenon that
refuses to be confined to any one side of the paradigm – tradition
and modernity, center and periphery, gay and straight.

Giving a new twist or shade to García Lorca's most famous line
of poetry, the lesbian and gay students' group of Madrid's
Complutense University have named themselves "Rosa que te
quiero rosa" ("Pink how I love you, pink").[17] Beyond the continuing critical focus on such motifs as ritual sacrifice and the wounded
heart in García Lorca,[18] I suggest that more attention be paid to
such manifestations of love and of survival as those to be found in
the varied cases of Pasqual, Cortés, and "Rosa. . . ." While cultural
figures and activities of this kind that draw on García Lorca's legacy
will clearly have more cogency in Andalusia and the Spanish state,
a greater awareness of the challenge posed by García Lorca's
experimental drama may help to extend the reach of a putative
"García Lorca century" beyond Spain's borders, as Pasqual has
already attempted in such an exemplary fashion at the Théâtre de
l'Europe. The sometimes oblique but always fruitful engagement I

have traced here between García Lorca and Marañón, Hughes, Gide, and, finally, Freud is offered as a further step in this direction.

Conservative commentators, frightened by the rise of regionalism, have raised the question of "what remains of Spain."[19] García Lorca must be a primary example of a cultural remainder that will survive to be interpreted in new ways appropriate to the new and unfamiliar circumstances of a rightist government. But García Lorca's legacy can be read not as a testimony to the persistence of the nation-state and a national literature but rather as a pointer to their ruins. The García Lorca who staged the dance of the two Figures in *El público* in a Roman Ruin is also the García Lorca who shared with later gay Spanish writers a sense of "the disruptive and erotically transgressive potential in the landscape of ruins and classicism."[20] He may also have more than a little in common with the young Freud who experienced "A Disturbance of Memory on the Acropolis."[21] Succumbing to déjà vu before García Lorca's all-too-familiar literary monument, but also anxious (like Freud in Athens) not to outstrip our father if we go too far beyond him in our work of interpretation, surely we shall never abandon our first love. But we can attempt to rearticulate that nostalgic passion and maudlin cult of the past typical of the García Lorca legend as an ethics directed toward the future – as the affirmation of life in the face of mortality and the gift of the self to others in the risky but necessary passage from the subjective to the social.[22] Such are the ultimate implications (at once textual, performative, and psychoanalytic) of doing the theater of García Lorca.

Production Credits: Theater and Cinema

N.B.: Only press material cited in the text is listed here.

I. Theater

Chapter 1

Yerma, Madrid: Compañía Nuria Espert at the Teatro de la Comedia (1971).

Director	Víctor García
Production designer	Fabià Puigserver
Lighting designer	Polo Villaseñor
Yerma	Nuria Espert
Juan	José Luis Pellicena

ABC (1 December 1971).
El Alcázar (1 December 1971).
Gaceta Ilustrada (23 January 1972).
   (30 January 1972).
El Pueblo (30 November 1971).
Triunfo (5 February 1972).

Chapter 2

Bodas de sangre (*Bitter Oleander*), New York: Neighborhood Playhouse at the Lyceum Theater (1935).

Translator	José Weissberger
Director	Irene Lewisohn
Set design	Cleon Throckmorton, from sketches by Santiago Ontañón
Costumes	Polaire Weissman

Mother	Nance O'Neil
Novia	Eugenie Leontovich
Novio	Edgar Barrier
Leonardo	William Lawson

New York Evening Post (12 February 1935).
New York Herald Tribune (10 February 1935).
   (24 February 1935).
New York Sun (16 February 1935).
New York Telegraph (13 February 1935).
New York Times (12 February 1935).
New York World Telegram (12 February 1935).

Bodas de sangre (*Blood Wedding*), New York: The New York Shakespeare Festival at the Joseph Papp Public Theater/The Martinson Hall (1992).

Translator	Langston Hughes
Director	Melia Bensussen
Set designer	Derek McLane
Costumes	Franne Lee
Lighting designer	Peter Kaczorowski
Mother	Gloria Foster
Bride	Elizabeth Peña
Groom	Al Rodrigo
Leonardo	Joaquim de Almeida

New York (1 June 1992).
New York Times (15 May 1992).
Village Voice (26 May 1992).

Chapter 3

Así que pasen cinco años (*Lorsque cinq ans seront passés*), Paris: Théâtre Récamier (1958).

Translator and adaptor	Marcelle Auclair
Directors	Guy Suarès, Françoise Prévost

Production designer	Raymundo de Larrain
Young Man	Laurent Terzieff
Old Man	Jean-Marie Serreau
Typist	Pascale de Boysson
Fiancée	Nicole Desurmont

Les Arts (31 December 1958).
L'Aurore (29 December 1958).
Le Carrefour (31 December 1958).
Le Figaro (23 December 1958).
France Soir (25 December 1958).
L'Intransigeant (10 December 1958).
   (19 December 1958).
   (23 December 1958).
Les Lettres Francaises (4 December 1958).
   (1 January 1959).
Les Nouvelles Littéraires (22 January 1959).
Paris Journal (1 December 1958).
Le Parisien Libéré (4 December 1958).
   (26 December 1958).

Así que pasen cinco años: Madrid: TEC at the Teatro Eslava (1978).

Director	Miguel Narros
Production designer	José Hernández
Lighting designer	Francis Maniglia
Young Man	Manuel Angel Egea
Old Man	Guillermo Marín
Typist	Esperanza Roy
Fiancée	María Luisa San José

ABC (22 September 1978).
El País (21 September 1978).

Así que pasen cinco años, Madrid: Teatro Español (1989).

Director	Miguel Narros
Production designer	Andrea d'Odorico
Lighting designer	José Miguel López Sáez

Young Man	Carlos Hipólito
Old Man	Helio Pedregal
Typist	Ana Gracia
Fiancée	Cristina Marcos

ABC (30 April 1989).
El País (30 April 1989).

Chapter 4

El público, Madrid: Centro Dramático Nacional and Théâtre de l'Europe at the Teatro Nacional María Guerrero (1988) [first performed at the Piccolo Teatro in Milan (1986)].

Director	Lluís Pasqual
Production designer	Fabià Puigserver, in collaboration with Frederic Amat
Still photography	Ros Ribas

Director	Alfredo Alcón
First Man	Joan Miralles
Figure of Bells	Angel Pardo
Figure of Vine Leaves	Vicente Díez
Julieta	Maruchi León

ABC (12 December 1986).
  (8 April 1988).
  (12 June 1988).

II. Cinema (Chapter 4)

A. Adaptations

Bodas de sangre (1981)

Director	Carlos Saura
Choreographer	Antonio Gades
Production company	TVE
Director of photography	Teo Escamilla
Editor	Pablo G. del Amo

Leonardo	Antonio Gades
Novia	Cristina Hoyos
Novio	Juan Antonio Jiménez
Mother	Pilar Cardenas

ABC (26 June 1984).
El Correo Catalán (3 April 1981).
Informaciones (11 May 1983).
El País (11 May 1983).
La Vanguardia (25 March 1981).
  (27 March 1981).

La casa de Bernarda Alba (1987)

Director	Mario Camus
Production company	Paraíso Films, in collaboration with TVE
Screenplay	Mario Camus, Antonio Larreta
Director of photography	Fernando Arribas
Editor	José M. Biurrun
Bernarda	Irene Gutiérrez Caba
Adela	Ana Belén
Angustias	Enriqueta Carbelleira
Martirio	Victoria Peña

La Nueva España (14 April 1987).
El Periódico (23 November 1986).
  (14 April 1987).
  (15 April 1987).
La Vanguardia (21 April 1987).
Ya (8 April 1987).

B. Educational and biographical

El balcón abierto (1984)

| Director | Jaime Camino |
| Production company | TVE/Tibidabo Films |

Screenplay	José María Caballero Bonald, Jaime Camino
Director of photography	Juan Amorós
Editor	Teresa Alcocer
Voice of the Poet	José Luis Gómez
El Amargo/Leonardo	Antonio Flores
La niña amarga/Adela	Amparo Muñoz
Mother	Berta Riaza

Lorca, muerte de un poeta (1987)

Director	J. A. Bardem
Production company	TVE
Screenplay	J. A. Bardem, based on the books of Ian Gibson, with extracts from the works of Federico García Lorca
Director of photography	Hans Burmann
Editor	Guillermo S. Maldonado
García Lorca	Nicholas Grace
Ruiz Alonso	Angel de Andrés López

Notes

Introduction: Text, Performance, Psychoanalysis

1. The most recent symposium is "Teatro, Sociedad, y Política en la España de Siglo XX," 6–10 May 1996. The Fundación's journal has frequently devoted special sections to Spanish poets and playwrights other than García Lorca, such as Valle Inclán. So catholic is its range of contributors that it even includes one short piece by a former Francoist minister: Manuel Fraga Iribarne, "Mil primaveras más para Cunqueiro," *Boletín de la Fundación Federico García Lorca*, 15 (1994), 13–14.
2. I cite an anonymous text on the back of the Huerta's publicity leaflet, dated 1995 and published under the auspices of the Ayuntamiento de Granada.
3. The Casa-Museo Federico García Lorca in Fuentevaqueros is administered by the Diputación Provincial de Granada.
4. Alejandro V. García, "Lorca y Granada sellan la reconciliación con la apertura del Museo de la Huerta de San Vicente," *El País* (11 May 1995).
5. David Johnston, "Las terribles aduanas: The Fortunes of Spanish Theatre in English," *Donaire*, 1 (September 1993), 18–24 (p. 21).
6. "Lorca and Foucault," in *The Body Hispanic: Gender and Sexuality in Spanish and Spanish American Literature* (Oxford: Oxford University Press, 1989), 105–37 (pp. 106–9). It is to distance myself from the cult of "Lorca" and to call attention to the author function that I use the full name "García Lorca" throughout this book.
7. "La verdad de la vida: Gibson versus Lorca," *Boletín de la Fundación Federico García Lorca*, 4 (1988), 87–101 (p. 92).
8. See Helen Graham and Jo Labanyi (eds.), *Spanish Cultural Studies: An Introduction* (Oxford: Oxford University Press, 1995), p. 1.
9. Helen Graham and Jo Labanyi, "Culture and Modernity: The Case of Spain," in *Spanish Cultural Studies: An Introduction*, pp. 1–19 (p. 7).
10. Graham and Labanyi, p. 70 (picture caption). This comment is made in connection with Ernesto Giménez Caballero's "Cartel literario" dedicated to García Lorca, which includes experimental drawings and popular *aleluyas* and folkloric images.

11. For a collection of Spanish-language performance studies committed to a critique of text and traditional theater, see Diana Taylor and Juan Villegas (eds.), *Negotiating Performance: Gender, Sexuality, and Theatricality in Latin/o America* (Durham, N.C.: Duke University Press, 1995). For new approaches to text in Spanish theater of the 1980s, see Antonio Fernández Lera (ed.), *Nuevas tendencias escénicas: la escritura teatral a debate* (Madrid: Ministerio de Cultura, 1985).

12. *Prosa inédita de juventud*, ed. Christopher Maurer; *Teatro inédito de juventud*, ed. Andrés Soria Olmedo; *Poesía inédita de juventud*, ed. Christian de Paepe; all three published in Madrid by Cátedra in 1994. In his introduction Maurer writes that the delay in publication was caused by him as editor rather than by García Lorca's family, as was widely believed (p. 51).

13. Javier Ruiz Portella (ed.), *Sonetos del amor oscuro; Poemas de amor y erotismo; Inéditos de madurez* (Barcelona: Altera, 1995).

14. Antonio Monegal (ed.), *Viaje a la luna* (Valencia: Pre-textos, 1994).

15. The English version is Rafael Martínez Nadal, *Lorca's "The Public": A Study of His Unfinished Play ("El Público") and of Love and Death in the Work of Federico García Lorca* (London: Calder and Boyars, 1974).

16. *García Lorca en el teatro: la norma y la diferencia* (Zaragoza: Universidad de Zaragoza, 1986), p. 278.

17. The *Boletín de la Fundación Federico García Lorca* has devoted two special sections to *Así que pasen cinco años* and avant-garde theater: 6 (1989), 11–86; 7–8 (1990), 197–256.

18. Phyllis Hartnoll (ed.), *Oxford Companion to the Theatre*, 4th ed. (Oxford: Oxford University Press, 1995), p. 314, s.v. "García Lorca, Federico."

19. See the introduction of that title to the volume edited by Silvia L. López, Jenaro Talens, and Darío Villanueva, *Critical Practices in Post-Franco Spain* (Minneapolis: University of Minnesota Press, 1994).

20. One early feminist reading is Julianne Burton's "'The Greatest Punishment': Female and Male in Lorca's Tragedies," in *Women in Hispanic Literature* (Berkeley: University of California Press), pp. 259–79. An early gay reading is Paul Binding's *Lorca: The Gay Imagination* (London: GMP, 1985); Carlos Jerez Ferrán has been working for some time on a gay-themed study of García Lorca – he kindly showed me several chapters, one of which reads *El público* in the light of Marañón's theory of intersexuality; this was written before my reading of *Yerma*, which also cites Marañón. Luis Fernández Cifuentes's work combines sophisticated deconstructive argument with historical scholarship in an exemplary way. Antonio Monegal's recent "Unmasking the Masculine: Transvestism and Tragedy in García Lorca *El público*," *MLN*, 109

(1994), 204–16, rehearses the deconstructive topoi of the mask and performance.

21. Melia Bensussen, "Introduction," in *Blood Wedding and Yerma* (New York: TCG, 1994), pp. vii–xiii (p. xi).

22. See Andrés Amorós, "Problemas para el estudio del teatro español del siglo XX," in Dru Dougherty and María Francisca Vilches de Frutos (eds.), *El teatro en España: entre la tradición y la vanguardia (1918–39)* (Madrid: Tabapress, 1992), pp. 19–22 (p. 19), and Moisés Pérez Coterillo, "La escritura teatral: marco para un debate," in Antonio Fernández Lera (ed.), *Nuevas tendencias escénicas: la escritura teatral a debate* (Madrid: Ministerio de Cultura, 1985), pp. 14–20 (pp. 18, 19). According to statistics reproduced here in May 1984, only 6.94 percent of the productions by professional theater groups in Spain were by twentieth-century Spanish dramatists who were no longer living, such as García Lorca and Valle Inclán; foreign dramatists in that category were almost twice as likely to be performed in Spain.

23. Sue Frenk, Chris Perriam, and Mike Thompson, "The Literary Avant-garde: A Contradictory Modernity," in Helen Graham and Jo Labanyi (eds.), *Spanish Cultural Studies: An Introduction,* pp. 63–70 (p. 65).

24. Although I concentrate on Paris here, the period from 1958 ("les années Malraux") marked a decentralization of French theater linked to the creation of regional Maisons de la Culture; see Robert Abirached (ed.), *La Décentralisation théâtrale* (Bourges: Actes du Sud, 1996).

25. The program is produced by the Centro Dramático Nacional for the 1987–8 season. For a full selection of Amat's paintings and his unrealized project with Puigserver for a traveling theater, see Frederic Amat, *El teatro de Federico García Lorca: obras sobre papel de Frederic Amat para un proyecto de Frederic Amat y Fabià Puigserver* (Granada: Diputación Provincial de Granada, 1988).

26. John Hooper, *The New Spaniards* (London: Penguin, 1995), p. 327.

27. In a publicity pullout in the Madrid listing magazine *Guía del Ocio* celebrating the tenth anniversary of the CNTC, Alberto de la Hera writes that both the public and the critics had "turned their backs" on Spanish classical theater until the founding of the Centre; "Un afortunado cumpleaños," in *Guía del Ocio: especial CNTC* (no date [1996]), p. 3.

28. The patient is "Anna O."; see Josef Breuer, "Case 1: Fräulein Anna O.," in *Studies in Hysteria,* Penguin Freud Library 2 (London: Penguin, 1991), pp. 73–102 (p. 74).

29. Lisa Appignanesi and John Forrester, "Freud on Trial," in *Freud's Women* (London: Virago, 1992), pp. 1–7.

30. Alan Sinfield, *The Wilde Century: Effeminacy, Oscar Wilde, and the Queer Moment* (London: Cassell, 1994), p. 166.

31. Jeremy Tambling, *Confession: Sexuality, Sin, the Subject* (Manchester, England: Manchester University Press, 1990), p. 182.

32. "Hysterical Phantasies and Bisexuality," in *On Psychopathology*, Penguin Freud Library 10 (London: Penguin, 1993), pp. 83–94 (pp. 93, 94).

33. "Mourning and Melancholia," in *On Metapsychology*, Penguin Freud Library 11 (London: Penguin, 1991), pp. 245–68.

34. "The Economic Problem of Masochism," in *On Metapsychology*, pp. 409–26 (p. 420).

35. *Case Histories I*, Penguin Freud Library 8 (London: Penguin, 1990), p. 41.

36. Here I have inverted Freud, whose "remarkable thing" is "a feminine attitude without a homosexual object choice" in male beating fantasies; "'A Child Is Being Beaten': A Contribution to the Study of the Origin of Sexual Perversions," in *On Psychopathology*, pp. 159–93 (p. 187).

37. Martínez Nadal, *Lorca's The Public*, p. 219, 220.

38. On the one hand, a schoolchildren's commentary to a García Lorca play repeatedly mentions the author's homosexuality: Cristina Serrano Carrasco, *La casa de Bernarda Alba*, Apuntes Cúpula (Barcelona: CEAC, 1989); on the other, the editor of the first edition of the *Sonetos del amor oscuro* dismisses the possibility that the sonnets make even a "veiled allusion" to homosexuality (p. 10), intersperses them with line drawings of female nudes, and juxtaposes them with well-known poems such as *La casada infiel*, whose theme (unlike that of the *Sonetos*) is explicitly heterosexual. Rarely has the disavowal of García Lorca's homosexuality been so insistent.

39. Gwynne Edwards (trans.), *Plays Two* (London: Methuen, 1990), p. xiii.

40. *Looking for Langston* (UK, 1989).

41. See Marcelle Auclair, *Enfances et mort de García Lorca* (Paris: Seuil, 1968), pp. 194, 201.

42. *Prosa inédita de juventud*, pp. 32, 34, 35.

43. *Prosa inédita de juventud*, pp. 459–62.

44. "Fonction et champ de la parole et du langage en psychanalyse," in *Ecrits I* (Paris: Seuil, 1966), pp. 111–208 (p. 177).

45. Graham and Labanyi, "Introduction," *Spanish Cultural Studies*, p. 14.

1. Yerma and the Doctors: García Lorca, Marañón, and the Anxiety of Bisexuality

1. Guadalupe Martinez Lacalle, "*Yerma*: 'Una tragedia pura y simplemente,'" *Neophilologus*, 72 (1988), 227–37 (p. 235).

2. John Gilmour, "The Cross of Pain and Death: Religion in the Rural Tragedies," in Robert Havard (ed.), *Lorca: Poet and Playwright* (Cardiff: University of Wales, 1992), pp. 133–55 (p. 144).

3. Fiona Parker and Terence McMullan, "Federico García Lorca's *Yerma* and the World of Work," *Neophilologus*, 74 (1990), pp. 58–69 (p. 67).

4. Robert Lima, "Towards the Dionysiac: Pagan Elements and Rites in *Yerma*," in Manuel Durán and Francesca Colecchia (eds.), *Lorca's Legacy: Essays on Lorca's Life, Poetry, and Theatre* (New York: Peter Lang, 1991), pp. 115–34 (p. 118).

5. Ildefonso-Manuel Gil, *Yerma*, 2nd ed. (Madrid: Cátedra, 1976), p. 28.

6. Robin Warner (ed.), *Yerma* (Manchester, England: Manchester University Press, 1994), p. 13.

7. Luis Fernández Cifuentes, "*Yerma:* anatomía de una transgresión," *MLN*, 99 (1984), 288–307 (p. 305).

8. Robin Warner, p. 12.

9. "Types of Onset of Neurosis," in *On Psychopathology* (London: Penguin, 1993), pp. 115–27 (p. 127).

10. Ian Gibson, *Federico García Lorca* (Barcelona: Grijalbo, 1987), II, pp. 335, 439.

11. Gibson, p. 337.

12. Gibson, pp. 334, 337, 338.

13. *Los estados intersexuales en la especie humana* (Madrid: Javier Morata, 1929), unnumbered. This is typical of the parallels I will be drawing between the practices of theater and of medicine. By juxtaposing García Lorca and Marañón I argue not that the latter's texts are an interpretive key to the former's but rather that, in their similarities and differences, these two contemporaneous views of sexuality can productively be read as implicit commentaries on each other.

14. *Medicina española contemporánea* (Salamanca: Universidad, 1986), pp. 56, 188, 193, 198.

15. *La mujer como profesional de la medicina en la España del siglo XIX* (Barcelona: Anthropos, 1988), pp. 171–95.

16. *Estudio higiénico-médico de las casas de maternidad* (Madrid: R. Velasco, 1893).

17. Cited by Soler in his "La maternidad" in *Discursos leídos en la Sociedad Española de Higiene en la sesión inaugural del año académico de 1936* (Madrid: J. Cosano, 1936), 21–33 (p. 32).

18. *Embarazo, parto, y puerperio* (Madrid: Ducazcal, 1904), pp. 8, 12.

19. *Preceptos acerca del embarazo, parto, y puerperio* (Barcelona: J. Horta, 1909), pp. 4, 5, 6.

20. "Conducta del ginecólogo ante la esterilidad femenina," *Anales de la Real Academia Nacional de Medicina*, 47 (1927), pp. 421–32.

21. The surgeon is León Cardenal; reproduced in Granjel, p. 188.

22. *La esterilidad en la mujer: ¿qué causas la originan?* (Madrid: Morata, 1941), pp. 9, 48.
23. "La maternidad," pp. 21, 22, 23, 25.
24. Ed. Robin Warner (Manchester, England: Manchester University Press, 1994), I, 1, 40.
25. Avila de Lobera, *Libro del régimen de la salud y de la esterilidad de los hombres y mujeres* (Madrid: Julio Cosano, 1923), pp. 170, 187.
26. Joseph Ventura Pastor, *Discurso médico chirúrgico sobre los depósitos lácteos o leche extraviada en las mugeres embarazadas* (Madrid: Viuda de Ibarra, 1793).
27. "La esterilidad," p. 423.
28. *La esterilidad en la mujer,* p. 13.
29. *The Significance and Impact of Gregorio Marañón* (New York: Bilingual Press, 1977), pp. 21–2.
30. Pedro Laín Entralgo, *Gregorio Marañón: vida, obra, y persona* (Madrid: Espasa Calpe, 1969 [first ed. 1966]), p. 169.
31. *La polémica feminista en España contemporánea* (Madrid: Akal, 1986), p. 185.
32. Warner argues that in *Yerma* García Lorca "does not challenge accepted definitions of culture" and is "positively supportive of traditional prescriptions" (pp. 5, 17).
33. See, for example, Ildefonso-Manuel Gil, *Yerma,* 2nd ed. (Madrid: Cátedra, 1976), p. 29.
34. *El problema social de la infección* (Madrid: El Libro del Pueblo, 1929), p. 48.
35. *Tres ensayos sobre la vida sexual,* 3rd ed. (Madrid: Biblioteca Nueva, 1927), p. 55; see also *Amor, conveniencia, y eugenesia* (Madrid: Historia Nueva, 1929).
36. *Biología y feminismo* (Madrid: Sucesor de Enrique Teodoro, 1920), p. 9.
37. *Patología e higiene de la emoción* (Madrid: Sucesor de Enrique Teodoro, 1925), p. 4.
38. *Climaterio de la mujer y del hombre* (Madrid: Espasa Calpe, 1937), pp. 165, 168.
39. *Amiel: un estudio sobre la timidez,* 6th ed. (Madrid: Espasa Calpe, 1941), passim.
40. *Los estados intersexuales en la especie humana* (Madrid: Javier Morata, 1929), p. x.
41. Paul Binding, *Lorca: The Gay Imagination* (London: GMP, 1985), pp. 173–8.
42. Cited by Julio Huélamo Kosma, "La influencia de Freud en el teatro de García Lorca," *Boletín de la Fundación Federico García Lorca,* 6 (1989), 59–83 (p. 61).

43. Cited by Laín, p. 98.
44. J. Laplanche and J. B. Pontalis, *The Language of Psychoanalysis* (London: Karnak, 1988), p. 53.
45. "On the Grounds for Detaching a Particular Syndrome from Neurasthenia under the Description 'Anxiety Neurosis,'" in *On Psychopathology* (London: Penguin, 1993), pp. 31–66.
46. "My Views on the Part Played by Sexuality in the Etiology of the Neuroses," pp. 67–82.
47. "Hysterical Fantasies and Their Relation to Bisexuality," pp. 83–94.
48. "Some General Remarks on Hysterical Attacks," pp. 95–102.
49. "The Disposition to Obsessional Neurosis," pp. 129–44.
50. "A Child Is Being Beaten (A Contribution to the Study of the Origin of Sexual Perversions)," pp. 159–94. For sadism, see also "Some Neurotic Mechanisms in Jealousy, Paranoia, and Homosexuality," pp. 195–208.
51. "Estreno de *Yerma*," *El Pueblo* (30 November 1971).
52. "*Yerma:* forma y contenido," *Triunfo* (5 February 1972).
53. See, for example, anon., "*Yerma* de Víctor García, en la Comedia," *ABC* (1 December 1971).
54. Anon., "*Yerma* en versión de Víctor García," *El Alcázar* (1 December 1971).
55. "Resurrección de *Yerma*," *Gaceta Ilustrada* (23 January 1972).
56. "El drama de *Yerma*," *Gaceta Ilustrada* (30 January 1972).
57. See Alberto Miralles, "La progresiva domesticación de la vanguardia teatral durante la transición política española," in Antonio Fernández Lera (ed.), *Nuevas tendencias escénicas: la escritura teatral a debate* (Madrid: Ministerio de Cultura, 1985), pp. 26–30.
58. The production was by London Classic Theatre Company at Southwark Playhouse; see Jane Clinton's review in *Time Out* (13–20 September 1995), which singles out Juan's "homosexual encounter with Víctor" for special praise.
59. "Some Neurotic Mechanisms in Jealousy, Paranoia, and Homosexuality," in *On Psychopathology* (London: Penguin, 1993), pp. 195–208 (p. 201).
60. "Ensayo liminar," *Tres ensayos*, pp. 11–22 (p. 20).
61. *The History of Sexuality: An Introduction* (New York: Vintage, 1978), p. 55.

2. Black Wedding: García Lorca, Langston Hughes, and the Translation of Introjection

1. Andrew A. Anderson's important "Strategy of García Lorca's Dramatic Composition 1930–36," *Romance Quarterly*, 33 (1986), 211–29,

addresses this question in the broader context of the drama as a whole.

2. Leslie Stainton's "A Concept of Land: José Luis Gómez, Lorca, and *Bodas de sangre*," *Anales de la Literatura Española Contemporánea,* 11 (1986), pp. 205–13, documents a production staged in and drawing on this region.

3. Reed Anderson, "The Idea of Tragedy in García Lorca's *Bodas de sangre,*" *Revista Hispánica Moderna,* 38 (1974–5), 174–88.

4. Sumner M. Greenfield, "Lorca's Tragedies: Practice without Theory," *Siglo XX/20th Century,* 4.1–2 (1986–7), 1–5.

5. Christopher Maurer is preparing "a full study of the [Weissberger] translation and New York production" based on manuscripts in the Billy Rose Theater Collection of the New York Public Library; see "Bach and *Bodas de sangre,*" in Manuel Durán and Francesca Colecchia (eds.), *Lorca's Legacy* (New York: Peter Lang, 1991), pp. 103–14 (p. 112, n. 16). One valuable item in the collection not listed by Maurer in this note is the actress Nance O'Neil's scrapbook (Call No. MWEZ X n.c. 1987). Maurer is not concerned with Hughes's translation, which is bound with Weissberger's (Call No. NCOF p.v. 359). Brief published accounts of the New York production can be found in the introduction to Mario Hernández's edition of *Bodas de sangre* (Madrid: Alianza, 1984), pp. 56–62; Ian Gibson, *Federico García Lorca* (Barcelona: Grijalbo, 1987), II, pp. 77, 343; and María Francisca Vilches de Frutos and Dru Dougherty, *Los estrenos teatrales de Federico García Lorca* (Madrid: Tabapress, 1992), p. 77. For García Lorca's own response to New York theater and its influence on his subsequent work, see Andrew A. Anderson, "On Broadway, Off Broadway: García Lorca and the New York Theater 1929–30," *Gestos: Teoría y Práctica del Teatro Hispánico,* 16 (1993), 135–48; and Sumner M. Greenfield, "El poeta de vuelta en España: lo neoyorquino en el teatro de Lorca, 1933–36," *Boletín de la Fundación de Federico García Lorca,* 10–11 (1992), 85–93. See also Luis Fernández Cifuentes, "Lorca en Nueva York: arquitecturas para un poeta," *Boletín de la Fundación de Federico García Lorca,* 10–11 (1992), 125–35.

6. Melia Bensussen, the director of the production of Hughes's translation, has published a version of the text based on Hughes's first draft and adapted by her company in rehearsal: *Blood Wedding and Yerma* (New York: TCG, 1994). I cite Hughes's typescript of the second draft, which Bensussen has not seen (see below).

7. Hughes translated both *Bodas de sangre* and the *Romancero gitano;* gave a radio talk on García Lorca in 1938, when he was a correspondent for African American newspapers in Madrid; proposed a book of Gar-

cía Lorca translations to his publisher in 1946; and taught texts by García Lorca when he was a visiting professor at Atlanta University in 1948. See Arnold Rampersad's authorized biography, *The Life of Langston Hughes* (Cambridge: Cambridge University Press, 1986–8), I, pp. 341, 350, 352, II, pp. 106, 120, 128. See also Faith Berry's unauthorized *Langston Hughes: Before and Beyond Harlem* (Westport, Conn.: Lawrence Hill, 1983), pp. 260, 267, 321.

8. See Arnold Rampersad, "Langston Hughes and His Critics on the Left," *Langston Hughes Review*, 5.2 (1986), 34–40.

9. Rampersad claims that Hughes was not gay, based on his inability to identify Hughes's male lovers and the claim that Hughes's work is "virtually devoid of pieces that even hint at an interest in homosexuality" (II, 333–6). One quite explicit piece Rampersad fails to quote in this context is "Café 3 A.M." ("God, Nature, or somebody made [fairies] that way"), which Hughes chose to reprint in his *Selected Poems* of 1959 (my edition: London: Pluto, 1986), p. 243. For a homoerotic "Meditation on Langston Hughes and the Harlem Renaissance," see Isaac Julien's short film made for UK Channel 4 TV, *Looking for Langston* (1989).

10. See "Winter Moon," "Gypsy Melodies," "Young Sailor," and "Ballad of the Gypsy," in *Selected Poems* (pp. 58, 64, 73, 124). "The Negro Speaks of Rivers" (p. 4), an assertion of African continuity, is Hughes's best-known early poem. This collection also reprints poems on the theme of unsatisfied desire ("Lament over Love," pp. 143–56); written in a first-person female voice ("Madam to You," pp. 201–20); and overtly political in nature ("Words Like Freedom," pp. 275–97).

11. Ian Gibson, *Federico García Lorca* (Barcelona: Grijalbo, 1987), II, pp. 77–8.

12. See José Ortega, "El gitano y el negro en la poesía de García Lorca," *Cuadernos Hispanoamericanos*, 433–4 (1986), 145–68; Miguel Enguídanos, "Del rey de los gitanos al rey de Harlem: sobre *Poeta en Nueva York*," *Insula*, 476–7 (July–August 1986), pp. 145–68.

13. Carlos Feal, "El sacrificio de la hombría en *Bodas de sangre*," *MLN*, 99 (1984), 270–87.

14. "Mourning and Melancholia" and "The Economic Problem of Masochism," in *On Metapsychology* (Harmondsworth: Penguin, 1984), pp. 245–68 and 409–26, respectively. I also cite "Negation" from the same volume (pp. 435–42).

15. J. Laplanche and J. B. Pontalis, *The Language of Psychoanalysis* (London: Karnac, 1988), pp. 211, 229.

16. *Broadway* (London: Cassell, 1970), pp. 414–15. Atkinson continued to write reviews into the 1960s; his review is not cited by Hernández,

whose sketch of New York notices remains the most detailed account of *Bodas de sangre*'s reviews.

17. Daniel Blum, *A Pictorial History of the American Theater 1860–1976*, enlarged and revised by John Willis (New York: Crown, 1977), p. 267.

18. See Morgan Y. Himelstein, *Drama Was a Weapon: The Left-Wing Theater in New York 1929–41* (New Brunswick, N.J.: Rutgers University Press, 1963), p. 37; and more recently Andrew B. Harris, *Broadway Theater* (London and New York: Routledge, 1994), pp. 26–33 (esp. p. 30).

19. "Trouble with the Angels," pp. 6–7. The piece documents an attempted strike by the cast to protest against playing to segregated audiences.

20. Mary C. Henderson, *The City and the Theater: New York Playhouses from Bowling Green to Times Square* (Clifton, N.J.: James T. White, 1973).

21. *The Neighborhood Playhouse* (New York: Theater Arts, 1959), pp. xiii–xiv.

22. *The Neighborhood Playhouse*, p. 243.

23. I cite this review from Nance O'Neil's scrapbook, where no source is given.

24. Blum, *A Pictorial History of the American Theater;* O'Neil, pp. 57, 81, 163, 180; Leontovich, pp. 246, 298, 348.

25. Federico García Lorca, *Three Plays*, trans. Michael Dewell and Carmen Zapata (Harmondsworth: Penguin, 1992), pp. xxvii–xxviii.

26. John F. Matheus, "Langston Hughes as Translator," in Therman B. O'Daniel (ed.), *Langston Hughes: Black Genius* (New York: William Morrow, 1971), pp. 157–70 (p. 157). Hughes also translated Nicolás Guillén and Gabriela Mistral. For the former see Richard Jackson, "The Shared Vision of Langston Hughes and Black Hispanic Writers," *Black American Literature Forum*, 15.3 (1981), 89–92. Jackson argues that Guillén and Hughes share "a commitment to radical change for the black masses" (p. 92). See also Edward Mullen, "Langston Hughes in Mexico and Cuba," *Review: Latin American Literature and Arts*, 47 (Fall 1993), pp. 23–7.

27. Hernández, ed. p. 58.

28. *Bodas de sangre*, ed. H. Ramsden (Manchester, England: Manchester University Press, 1980). I cite this edition by act, scene, and page numbers.

29. I cite the second of four versions bound together with the common Call No. NCOF p.v. 359: "Bodas de sangre/by/Federico García Lorca/Property of/The Neighborhood Playhouse . . ." This is the only version with light and sound cues, stage plans, and diagrams of actor movement. I cite this ms. by act, scene, and folio numbers. Text that has been crossed out is placed within square brackets.

30. This is the fourth version in the collection cited in note 29: "Bodas de sangre/(Second draft)/FATE AT THE WEDDING/A Play/by/Federico García Lorca." I cite by act, scene, and folio numbers.

31. The nature of Hughes's political commitment is disputed by some scholars; Samuel A. Hay finds "no evidence of social consciousness" in Hughes and no political effect in *Mulatto; African American Theatre* (Cambridge: Cambridge University Press, 1994), pp. 32, 84.

32. Edith J.R. Isaacs, *The Negro in the American Theatre* (New York: Theatre Arts, 1947), p. 96.

33. Arnold Rampersad, *The Life of Langston Hughes* (Cambridge: Cambridge University Press, 1986–8), I, pp. 191–2, 285, 312–20, 324, 327–8. Hughes treated the mulatto theme in drama, poetry, narrative, and, finally, as a libretto; see Sybil Ray Ricks, "A Textual Comparison of Langston Hughes's *Mulatto*, 'Father and Son,' and 'The Barrier,'" *Black American Literature Forum*, 15.3 (1981), 101–3. Hughes's versatility is stressed in an anonymous contemporary press report: "Langston Hughes Now Adds Drama to Other Mediums: He Already Has Conquered Novel and Poetry Forms, and Is a Translator, Too," *New York Herald Tribune* (24 November 1935).

34. The description is Edith J.R. Isaacs's in *The Negro in the American Theatre* (New York: Theatre Arts, 1947), caption to frontispiece portrait of Rose McClendon.

35. Father–son conflict has, however, been seen by one critic as central to García Lorca's writing as a whole; Javier Herrero, "The Father Against the Son: Lorca's Christian Vision," in Manuel Durán and Francesca Colecchia (eds.), *Lorca's Legacy* (New York: Peter Lang, 1991), pp. 1–20.

36. I cite the text published by Webster Smalley, in *Five Plays* (Bloomington: Indiana University Press, 1963), pp. 1–42. The published text is quite different from the mutilated version produced, most particularly in the absence of the rape of the young daughter inserted by the producer against Hughes's wishes.

37. Richard K. Barksdale, "Miscegenation on Broadway: Hughes's *Mulatto* and Edward Sheldon's *The Nigger*," in Edward J. Mullen (ed.), *Critical Essays on Langston Hughes* (Boston: G.K. Hall, 1986), pp. 191–9 (p. 194).

38. "Negation," p. 439.

39. Terence McMullen, "Federico García Lorca's Critique of Marriage in *Bodas de sangre*," *Neophilologus*, 77 (1993), pp. 61–73 (p. 71).

40. Carlos Feal, "El sacrificio de la hombría en *Bodas de sangre*," *MLN*, 99 (1984), 270–87.

41. Laplanche and Pontalis, p. 212.

42. Laplanche and Pontalis, p. 229.
43. See Ramsden's introduction to his edition, p. xxxiii.
44. Mel Gussow, "A García Lorca Tragedy of Blood Lust and Death," 15 May 1992.
45. John Simon, 1 June 1992.
46. Michael Feingold, "Bloody Poetry," 26 May 1992.
47. "Pragmatism and the Sense of the Tragic," in *Keeping Faith: Philosophy and Race in America* (New York and London: Routledge, 1993), pp. 107–18 (p. 114).
48. "Nihilism in Black America," in *Race Matters* (Boston: Beacon, 1992), pp. 11–20 (pp. 11–13).
49. "Pragmatism and the Sense of the Tragic," pp. 109, 115.
50. See West on jazz as cultural hybrid, "Malcolm X and Black Rage," in *Race Matters*, pp. 95–105 (pp. 104–5).
51. *Five Lectures on Psychoanalysis* (London: Penguin, 1995), p. 17.
52. For the supposed antithesis between a "telluric" Andalusia and a "materialist" North America, see Allen Josephs and Juan Caballero's introduction to their edition of *Bodas de sangre* (Madrid: Cátedra, 1985), p. 47.
53. Andrew A. Anderson notes that for García Lorca the third play in his trilogy was not *La casa de Bernarda Alba* but the Biblical play known variously as *Las hijas de Lot* or *La destrucción de Sodoma;* "The Strategy of García Lorca's Dramatic Composition 1930–36," *Romance Quarterly,* 33 (1986), 211–29 (p. 218); John K. Walsh notes that García Lorca's "previous works [to *Bodas de sangre* were] written on homosexuality"; "A Genesis for García Lorca's *Bodas de sangre*," *Hispania,* 74 (1991), 255–61 (p. 255).
54. C. B. Morris cites "the black gown formerly worn for a wedding in Galicia at least"; *Bodas de sangre* (London: Grant and Cutler, 1980), p. 54.

3. Poet in Paris: Así que pasen cinco años *(When Five Years Have Passed),* Corydon, *and the Truth of Anamnesis*

1. I cite throughout the critical edition by Margarita Ucelay, *Así que pasen cinco años: leyenda del tiempo* (Madrid: Cátedra, 1995); an English translation is available by Gwynne Edwards in García Lorca, *Plays 2* (London: Methuen, 1990), pp. 123–81. Translations in this chapter are my own.
2. Ucelay, p. 66. See also Virginia Higginbotham, "*Así que pasen cinco años:* A Literary Version of *Un Chien andalou*," in Manuel Durán and

Francesca Colecchia (eds.), *Lorca's Legacy: Essays on Lorca's Life, Poetry, and Theater* (New York: Peter Lang, 1991), pp. 195–204 (p. 197); and Josef W. Zdenek, "Alter Ego and Personality Projection in García Lorca's *Así que pasen cinco años*," *Revista de Estudios Hispánicos*, 16 (1982), pp. 303–13. Joaquín Roses-Lozano stresses "three levels of construction" in "Códigos sígnicos y discurso teatral en *Así que pasen cinco años*," *Anales de la Literatura Española Contemporánea*, 14 (1989), 115–41 (p. 116).

3. Ucelay, p. 117. For exterior as interior see also Andrew A. Anderson, "*El público, Así que pasen cinco años, y El sueño de la vida:* tres dramas expresionistas de García Lorca," in Dru Dougherty and María Francisca Vilches de Frutos (eds.), *El teatro en España: entre la tradición y la vanguardia* (Madrid: Tabapress, 1992), pp. 215–26 (p. 220).

4. See Anderson, "*El público, Así que pasen cinco años, y El sueño de la vida*" (cited in note 3) for a convincing argument against the excessively frequent and unexamined designation of García Lorca's experimental dramas as "surrealist" (p. 215 and passim).

5. Ucelay, p. 45; see Julio Huélamo Kosma, "La influencia de Freud en el teatro de García Lorca," *Boletín de la Fundación Federico García Lorca*, 6 (1989), 59–83 (p. 75).

6. Huélamo, "La influencia," suggests both methods of influence but favors the latter (p. 75).

7. Josef Breuer, "Theoretical," in Sigmund Freud and Josef Breuer, *Studies on Hysteria*, Penguin Freud Library, Vol. 3 (London: Penguin, 1991), 259–33 (p. 321).

8. I take the phrase "the truth of the life" from Luis Fernández Cifuentes's excellent deconstructive review article on Ian Gibson's monumental biography; revised and enlarged version: "La verdad de la vida: Gibson versus Lorca," *Boletín de la Fundación Federico García Lorca*, 4 (1988), 102–13. My distinction between anecdote and allegory corresponds to some extent to Fernández Cifuentes's distinction here between "fact" and "detail."

9. *Federico y su mundo* (Madrid: Alianza, 1981), pp. 332, 333.

10. "Introducción," p. 34.

11. For Ucelay it is the "autobiographical" nature of the theme of sterility that shows the "sincerity" of the play and the "confessional character" of its "internal journey" (pp. 99, 107).

12. Ucelay puts a new spin on the familiar dialectic of authenticity and revelation by claiming that the "authentic García Lorca always wanted to avoid being unveiled" (p. 63). Reticence, rather than confession, thus becomes the truth of the subject.

13. I concentrate on *A la recherche de Lorca* (Neuchâtel: Baconnière, 1966); this is a revised and expanded version of the original *Federico García Lorca: l'homme, l'oeuvre* (Paris: Plon, 1956). Between the two editions Schonberg added his thesis of García Lorca's supposed syphilis and impotence, the main interpretative "key" in *A la recherche*, absent in *Federico García Lorca*.

14. *Enfances et Mort de García Lorca* (Paris: Seuil, 1968).

15. "Diálogo antisocrático sobre *Corydon*," in André Gide, *Corydon* (Madrid: Alianza, 1971), pp. 7–23. I have also consulted the French text, *Corydon: édition augmentée* (Paris: Gallimard, 1924).

16. Sigmund Freud, *Case Histories I: "Dora" and "Little Hans,"* Penguin Freud Library, Vol. 8 (London: Penguin, 1990). In this chapter I also cite the earlier case histories in Sigmund Freud and Josef Breuer, *Studies in Hysteria* (cited in note 7).

17. *Case Histories I*, p. 96.

18. Breuer, "Case 1: Fräulein Anna O.," in *Studies in Hysteria*, pp. 73–102 (p. 74).

19. This slip appears in *The Psychopathology of Everyday Life;* it is cited by Mary S. Gossy in *Freudian Slips: Woman, Writing, the Foreign Tongue* (Ann Arbor: University of Michigan Press, 1995), p. 85.

20. *Cross-Cultural Approaches to Theatre: The Spanish–French Connection* (Metuchen, N.J., and London: Scarecrow Press, 1994), p. 35.

21. Zatlin, p. 45.

22. *Les Idées esthétiques de Federico García Lorca* (Paris: Centre de Recherches Hispaniques, 1967), p. 7.

23. The claim is repeated in *A la recherche de Lorca*, p. 9.

24. *The Assassination of Federico García Lorca* (London: Penguin, 1983), pp. 224–9. Gibson describes how Schonberg's theory was eagerly taken up by a nationalist government anxious to exculpate itself for García Lorca's murder.

25. See, for example, p. 125.

26. See *Genèse de l'âme poétique* (Paris: Gallimard, 1961). For example, Weber claims of Hugo "we discovered, not without surprise, that all the themes [of his work] are rooted in a *single* childhood memory" (p. 91); or again "the work and life of Verlaine appear to be profoundly *logical* as soon as one has managed to untangle the themes" (p. 337; Weber's emphasis). Verlaine's theme is a "ruinous [male] statue" that foretells "the poet's destiny" (p. 297). Weber promises (or threatens) that the "thematic system" is not confined to French literature but is universally applicable (p. 553). See also his *Domaines thématiques* (Paris: Gallimard, 1963).

27. *Enfances et Mort* (cited above). Auclair is also the author and translator of Catholic devotional works, including the complete works of St. Teresa of Avila.

28. *Federico García Lorca: A Life* (London: Faber, 1989), pp. 360–1.

29. My approach is thus similar to Anderson's treatment of expressionist antecedents of García Lorca's experimental drama in "*El público, Así que pasen cinco años, y El sueño de la vida*" (cited above).

30. References are to the French edition, unless otherwise specified.

31. The "Culex," whose attribution to the young Virgil is now rejected, figures among the Minor Poems or "Appendix Vergiliana."

32. Freud references are to *Case Histories 1*, unless otherwise attributed.

33. *Studies on Hysteria*, p. 86.

34. García Lorca's phrase ("el teatro del porvenir"), cited by Ucelay, p. 11.

35. Lisa Appignanesi and John Forrester, *Freud's Women* (London: Weidenfeld and Nicholson, 1991), p. 167.

36. "Lorca, todo Lorca, en una obra."

37. *Corydon*, pp. 61, 66.

38. Jane Gallop, "Keys to Dora," in Charles Bernheimer and Claire Kahane (eds.), *In Dora's Case: Feminism, Hysteria, Feminism* (London: Virago, 1985), pp. 200–20 (p. 208).

39. *Shorter Oxford English Dictionary* (Oxford: Clarendon, 1993), s.v. anamnesis.

4. García Lorca and the Socialists: Subsidized Cinema, Pasqual's Public, and the Identification of Affect

1. For a reliable overview of the arts and media under the Socialists see John Hooper, *The New Spaniards*, revised edition (London: Penguin, 1995), pp. 289–370. For critical accounts of Socialist policy toward cinema production see Augusto M. Torres's sketch "The Film Industry: Under Pressure from the State and Television," in *Spanish Cultural Studies: An Introduction: The Struggle for Modernity*, eds. Helen Graham and Jo Labanyi (Oxford: Oxford University Press, 1995), pp. 369–73; and John Hopewell's earlier and more extended *El cine español después de Franco* (Madrid: El Arquero, 1989), which cites the "disastrous" attempts to film literary classics in the context of a "national cinema" (p. 429). A minute description of government funding of cinema is found in Antonio Vallés Copeiro del Villa, *Historia de la política de fomento del cine español* (Valencia: Universidad, 1992). Telling examples of governmental aspirations in subsidizing theater and of theater professionals' often hostile response to the

same are to be found in the conference proceedings edited by Antonio Fernández Lera, *Nuevas tendencias escénicas: la escritura teatral a debate* (Madrid: Ministerio de Cultura/Dirección General de Música y Teatro, 1985).

2. Chávarri went on to make other films that reread Spanish history from a gay angle such as *Las cosas del querer* (1989), a fictionalized biography of Miguel de Molina, a popular singer and camp icon exiled since the Civil War.

3. See my *Laws of Desire: Questions of Homosexuality in Spanish Writing and Film 1960-90* (Oxford: Oxford University Press, 1992).

4. Copernico [*sic*], review of *A un dios desconocido*, *El Pueblo*, 28 September 1977.

5. Juan Tortella, review of *A un dios desconocido*, *El Pueblo de Mallorca*, 2 December 1977.

6. P.C., review of *A un dios desconocido*, *Ya*, 7 October 1977.

7. Published in English as: Ian Gibson, *Federico García Lorca: A Life* (London: Faber, 1989). *Lorca, muerte de un poeta* is a feature-length film edited down from Bardem's original TV series of the same title. Bardem is a veteran filmmaker with impeccable anti-Francoist credentials, known for such distinguished neo-realist works as *Muerte de un ciclista* (*Death of a Cyclist*, 1955).

8. Jaime Camino is known as a founder member of the "Barcelona school" whose films were frequently mutilated by the Francoist censor. His best-known film remains his personal account of the Civil War, *Las largas vacaciones del 36* (*The Long Holidays of 36*), 1975. *Dragon rapide* of 1986 returns to the same theme in a different context, marking the first time Franco and his wife had been played by actors in a Spanish film. See Augusto M. Torres, *Diccionario del cine español* (Madrid: Espasa Calpe, 1994), s.v. Camino and *Dragon rapide*. Torres dismisses *El balcón abierto* as "pretentious." See also Vicente Molina Foix's positive review of *Dragon rapide* in *El cine estilográfico: crítica recogida 1981-93* (Barcelona: Anagrama, 1993), p. 147.

9. The death sequences in both films also feature a voiceover reading lines from García Lorca's elegy for Ignacio Sánchez Mejías, thus implying that García Lorca had predicted his own death in this poem to another "distinguished Andalusian" ("un andaluz tan claro").

10. The standard book on Saura is Marvin D'Lugo's *The Films of Carlos Saura* (Princeton, N.J.: Princeton University Press, 1991). For Saura's work from 1975 to 1984 see Hopewell, *El cine*, pp. 243-79; on *Bodas de sangre* and *Carmen* in the context of a "national cinema," pp. 269-75. For *Bodas* as a document that transcends mere aestheticism (and Saura as the only Spanish director of his time to have achieved a

coherent career), see Vicente Molina Foix's review in *El cine estilográ-fico*, pp. 135–7.

11. A.P.G., "Lorca, Gades y Saura: *Bodas de sangre*," *Informaciones*, 11 May 1983.

12. L.B., "*Bodas de sangre:* la belleza del mito desnudo," *El País*, 11 May 1983.

13. Lluís Permanyer, "¡Acción!," *La Vanguardia*, 27 March 1981.

14. Muntañola [*sic*], "*Bodas de sangre*," *El Correo Cataláan*, 3 April 1981.

15. Angeles Maso, "*Bodas de sangre*," *La Vanguardia*, 25 March 1981.

16. One curious aspect of Saura's supposed fidelity to García Lorca that is not mentioned by the reviewers is the film's staging of a climactic, homoerotic dance of death between the two male protagonists, a final confrontation that is not shown in the original play, where it takes place off stage.

17. Efe, "*Bodas de sangre*, en el Festival del Cine Europeo," *ABC*, 26 June 1984.

18. For "quality" filmmaking and Miró sec Torres, "The Film Industry," p. 371; and Hopewell, *El cine*, pp. 394–408. The extensive government legislation attempting to support the film industry in the period of Miró's innovations (1987–90) is reprinted in Ferrán Alberich, *Cuatro años de cine español* (Madrid: Comunidad de Madrid/Consejería de Cultura, 1991), pp. 11–92. Official statistics show that these policies were not a success: from 1982 to 1989 the audience share taken by Spanish films in the domestic market fell from 30.2 percent to 7.7 percent, with the share of foreign films consequently rising from 69.8 percent to 92.3 percent.

19. See my *García Lorca/Almodóvar: Gender, Nationality, and the Limits of the Visible* (Cambridge: Cambridge University Press, 1995); reprinted and revised in *Vision Machines: Cinema, Literature, and Sexuality in Spain and Cuba, 1983–93* (London: Verso, 1996), pp. 17–36.

20. Antonio Lara, "Una imagen de la España eterna: *La casa de Bernarda Alba* de Mario Camus," *Ya*, 8 April 1987.

21. Gonzalo Pérez de Olaguer, "Un texto de siempre, también para siem-pre," *El Periódico*, 14 April 1987.

22. Pablo García, "Lorca permanece: *La casa de Bernarda Alba*," *La Nueva España*, 14 April 1987.

23. Jorge de Cominges, "La desgracia de ser mujer: *La casa de Bernarda Alba*," *El Periódico*, 15 April 1987.

24. Julio Fernández, "*La casa de Bernarda Alba* inicia su rodaje," *El Periódico*, 23 November 1986.

25. José Luis Guarner, "*La casa de Bernarda Alba*," *La Vanguardia*, 21 April 1987.

26. Anonymous, "Lluis Pasqual dejará el CDN para reincorporarse al Teatre Lliure," *ABC*, 4 March 1986. I thank María Delgado for kindly providing me with the press material on Pasqual.

27. Ignacio Buqueras y Bach, "Cataluña en Madrid: Marsillach-Pasqual," *ABC*, 12 June 1988.

28. S.C., "El público de Lorca," *Diario 16*, 27 June 1989.

29. Alejandro Pistolesi, "Milán, gran escenario del estreno mundial de *El público* de Federico García Lorca," *ABC*, 12 December 1986.

30. Juan Pedro Quiñonero, "Lluis Pasqual pisa el área de Jorge Lavelli: *El público* vuelve a la escena de París," *ABC*, 8 April 1988.

31. Juan Pedro Quiñonero, "Martirio y Ketama reinventan la tradición flamenca en París," *ABC*, 6 April 1988.

32. Efe, "Un desnudo teatral trae la polémica a la tranquila Turín," *ABC* 12 December 1986.

33. Ytak [*sic*], *Lluís Pasqual: Camí de teatre* (Barcelona: Alter Pirene Escene, 1994).

34. In the account of the production that follows, I draw on a videotape produced by the Spanish Ministerio de Cultura and the Instituto Nacional de las Artes Escénicas y de la Música kindly supplied to me by María Delgado; on my own memory of a performance on its Spanish tour in Seville; and on Ros Ribas's production photos in the program.

35. In the videotape Pasqual's credit as director is held on screen for nearly thirty seconds, considerably longer than García Lorca's.

36. Puigserver's work (including his design for *El público*) was the subject of an exhibition at the Centre Georges Pompidou in Paris in July 1995. He had earlier died of the effects of AIDS. The design for *El público* was in collaboration with the painter Frederic Amat.

37. For a clear account of quality and quantity with reference to the various accounts of affect, instinct, and idea in Freud see J. Laplanche and J.-B. Pontalis, *The Language of Psychoanalysis* (London: Karnac, 1988), s.v. "Affect." I discuss relevant aspects from two of Freud's essays later in this discussion of Pasqual's production.

38. In the introduction to her critical edition of the play (an essay some one hundred pages long), María Clementa Millán manages the considerable feat of never once mentioning the words "homosexual" or "homosexuality," although this topic has always been considered central to the play. I cite Millán's edition (Madrid: Cátedra, 1987) throughout. For homosexuality in *El público* and as "one of the four or five capital themes which run throughout the whole work of Lorca," see Rafael Martínez Nadal, *Lorca's "The Public": A Study of His Unfinished Play ("El Público") and of Love and Death in the Work of Federico García Lorca*

(London: Calder and Boyars, 1974), p. 31. Martínez Nadal is also a vigorous defender of García Lorca's "cultural load," so apparent in the allusive *El público* (p. 75).

39. Angel Pardo, the attractive actor who plays the Figure of Bells, had previously been cast by the maverick Basque film director Eloy de la Iglesia as a young hooligan in such exploitation films as *Los placeres ocultos* (*Hidden Pleasures*, 1976) and *El diputado* (*The MP*, 1978). De la Iglesia's homoerotic knife fights provide a piquant backdrop to García Lorca's amorous combats in this Cuadro.

40. In García Lorca's manuscript, "horses" replace "men" in the first Cuadro. See *Autógrafos: II: El público*, ed. Rafael Martínez Nadal (Oxford: Dolphin, 1976), p. 7.

41. In *On Psychopathology*, Penguin Freud Library 10 (London: Penguin, 1993), pp. 195–208. I also cite this essay in Chapter 1 of this book.

42. Jacques Lacan, "Le Stade du miroir comme formateur de la fonction du Je," in *Ecrits I* (Paris: Seuil, 1966), pp. 89–97 (p. 90).

43. In *On Metapsychology*, Penguin Freud Library 11 (London: Penguin, 1984), pp. 245–68. I also cite this essay in Chapter 2 of this book.

44. Compare the poem called "Crucifixión," which surrounds the central, tragic action with grotesque or ironic animal witnesses: dogs smoking pipes and cows with pellets or shot on their teats; Christopher Maurer (ed.), *Poet in New York* (London: Penguin, 1990), pp. 142–5.

45. Freud, "Mourning and Melancholia," p. 258.

46. Sigmund Freud, *The Interpretation of Dreams* (Harmondsworth: Penguin, 1976), pp. 231, 415–19.

47. Examples include Vicente Aranda's *Tiempo de silencio* (*Time of Silence*, 1986), based on the novel by Martín Santos; Francesc Betriu's *Réquiem por un campesino español* (*Requiem for a Spanish Peasant*, 1985), based on the novel by Sender; and Camus's own *Los santos inocentes* (*The Holy Innocents*, 1984), based on the novel by Delibes.

Conclusion: "Doing Lorca"

1. J.L. Tapia, "La Fundación García Lorca rechaza su traslado a Granada," *Ideal* (5 April 1996).

2. Natividad Pulido, "El Estado adquiere los textos inéditos de Lorca por casi cinco millones de pesetas: Alborch decidirá si van a la Biblioteca Nacional o a la Fundación del poeta," *ABC* (21 February 1995).

3. J.G.C., "El Ministerio de Cultura compra por 45 millones de pesetas el legado de Luis Buñuel," *ABC* (27 December 1995).

4. In the *Guardian*, references to García Lorca rose from nine in 1990 to twenty-five in 1994, before falling to eight in 1995; the figures for

Brecht are sixty-six, ninety-eight, and fifty, respectively. I have consulted *The Guardian on CD-ROM.*

5. Private communication with Benedict Carver, Madrid correspondent of *Screen International* (7 December 1995).

6. Antonio Gallego Morell, *Sobre García Lorca* (Granada: University of Granada, 1993), no page no. [introduction].

7. Darío Villanueva, "The Evolution of the Spanish Literary System," in José Colmeiro, Christina Dupláa, Patricia Greene, and Juana Sabadell (eds.), *Spain Today: Essays on Literature, Culture, Society* (Hanover, N.H.: Dartmouth College, 1995), pp. 139–47. Villanueva stresses the "stability" and "integration" of a system outsiders might accuse of inertia and introversion.

8. Amat has also made artworks on the theme of the body and AIDS such as "Anatomía." See my "Fatal Strategies: The Representation of AIDS in the Spanish State," in *Vision Machines: Cinema, Literature, and Sexuality in Spain and Cuba, 1983–93* (London: Verso, 1996), pp. 101–27 (p. 108).

9. The Teatro de la Danza was founded in 1979 and is well known for its productions of Gogol, Chekhov, Goethe, and Brecht, as well as for its stagings of director Luis Olmos's own fusions of dance and theater.

10. Ritama Muñoz-Rojas, "Lorca entra por primera vez en el teatro de La Latina," *El País* (17 September 1995).

11. Margot Molina, "Fría acogida en Sevilla al estreno de 'Haciendo Lorca' de Lluís Pasqual," *El País* (20 April 1996).

12. Rosana Torres, "El equipo de lujo de 'Haciendo Lorca' ofreció en Madrid el último estreno de la etapa socialista," *El País* (28 April 1996). One week earlier Alborch had attended the premiere of the biggest-budget Spanish film of the season, Vicente Aranda's *Libertarias,* an event that also had a nostalgic, Leftist atmosphere.

13. Itziar Pascual, "La escritura española de este siglo, apuesta del Centro Dramático Nacional," *El Mundo* (5 September 1995).

14. "Mourning and Melancholia," in *On Metapsychology,* Penguin Freud Library 11 (London: Penguin, 1991), pp. 245–68 (pp. 251, 252).

15. "The Psychogenesis of a Case of Homosexuality in a Woman," in *Case Histories II,* Penguin Freud Library 9 (London: Penguin, 1991), pp. 367–400 (p. 384).

16. Roger Salas, "Joaquín Cortés deslumbra con 'Pasión gitana': el espectáculo lleva el ballet flamenco hacia nuevos horizontes," *El País* (9 September 1995). Cortés is defined in this piece as a "bailarín-bailaor," the hyphenate suggesting his fusion of classical ballet and Andalusian popular tradition. Cortés, who played in Almodóvar's *La flor de mi secreto*

(*The Flower of My Secret*, 1995), subsequently took *Pasión* on a world tour.

17. "Rosa que te quiero rosa" can be reached at Aula 500, Facultad de Ciencias Políticas, Campus Somosaguas, Madrid.

18. David Johnston (ed. and trans.), *Yerma and the Love of Don Perlimplín for Belisa in the Garden* (London: Hodder and Stoughton, 1990), p. 3.

19. Federico Jiménez Losantos, *Lo que queda de España* (Madrid: Temas de Hoy, 1995). This revised edition by an *ABC* columnist contains a nostalgic retrospective of bohemian Barcelona in the 1970s and a dystopian prospective of a "Balcanic" Spain of the future.

20. One later writer is Luis Antonio de Villena; see Chris Perriam, *Desire and Dissent: An Introduction to Luis Antonio de Villena* (Oxford: Berg, 1995), p. 45. See also Villena's own "La sensibilidad homoerótica en el *Romancero gitano*," *Campus*, 11 (December 1986), 27–30. In spite of its title, this piece is illustrated, as is so often the case in Spain, with etchings that focus on female nudes.

21. "A Disturbance of Memory on the Acropolis," in *On Metapsychology*, Penguin Freud Library 11 (London: Penguin, 1991), pp. 443–56. In this late piece Freud remembers how he once felt among the ruins a sense of déjà vu that he attributes to an unconscious fear that he had outstripped his father, a man of commerce who would never visit Athens and would not have appreciated it if he had.

22. I take these themes from Fernando Savater's *Etica como amor propio* (Barcelona: Grijalbo Mondadori, 1995), passim.

Bibliography of Works Cited

N.B.: García Lorca texts are listed under the editor's name; press reviews of the main theatrical productions I examine in this book are listed under the appropriate heading in the "Production Credits" section, before this Bibliography.

Abirached, Robert (ed.), *La Décentralisation théâtrale* (Bourges: Actes du Sud, 1996).

Alberich, Ferrán, *Cuatro años de cine español* (Madrid: Comunidad de Madrid/Consejería de Cultura, 1991).

Alvarez Ricart, María del Carmen, *La mujer como profesional de la medicina en la España del siglo XIX* (Barcelona: Anthropos, 1988).

Amat, Frederic, *El teatro de Federico García Lorca: obras sobre papel de Frederic Amat para un proyecto de Frederic Amat y Fabià Puigserver* (Granada: Diputación Provincial de Granada, 1988).

Amorós, Andrés, "Problemas para el estudio del teatro español del siglo XX," in Dru Dougherty and María Francisca Vilches de Frutos (eds.), *El teatro en España: entre la tradición y la vanguardia (1918–39)* (Madrid: Tabapress, 1992), pp. 19–22.

Anderson, Andrew A., "The Strategy of García Lorca's Dramatic Composition 1930–36," *Romance Quarterly*, 33 (1986), 211–29.

"*El público, Así que pasen cinco años, y El sueño de la vida*: tres dramas expresionistas de García Lorca," in Dru Dougherty and María Francisca Vilches de Frutos (eds.), *El teatro en España: entre la tradición y la vanguardia* (Madrid: Taba Press, 1992), pp. 215–26.

"On Broadway, Off Broadway: García Lorca and the New York Theatre 1929–30," *Gestos: Teoría y Práctica del Teatro Hispánico*, 16 (1993), 135–48.

Anderson, Reed, "The Idea of Tragedy in García Lorca's *Bodas de sangre*," *Revista Hispánica Moderna*, 38 (1974–5), 174–88.

Anonymous, "Langston Hughes Now Adds Drama to Other Mediums: He Already Has Conquered Novel and Poetry Forms, and Is a Translator, Too," *New York Herald Tribune* (24 November 1935).

"Lluis Pasqual dejará el CDN para reincorporarse al Teatre Lliure," *ABC* (4 March 1986).

Appignanesi, Lisa, and John Forrester, *Freud's Women* (London: Weidenfeld and Nicholson, 1991).

Atkinson, Brooks, *Broadway* (London: Cassell, 1970).

Auclair, Marcelle, *Enfances et Mort de García Lorca* (Paris: Seuil, 1968).

Avila de Lobera, *Libro del régimen de la salud y de la esterilidad de los hombres y mujeres* (Madrid: Julio Cosano, 1923).

Aza, Vital, "Conducta del ginecólogo ante la esterilidad femenina," *Anales de la Real Academia Nacional de Medicina*, 47 (1927), 421–32.

La esterilidad en la mujer: ¿qué causas la originan? (Madrid: Morata, 1941).

Barksdale, Richard K., "Miscegenation on Broadway: Hughes's *Mulatto* and Edward Sheldon's *The Nigger*," in Edward J. Mullen (ed.), *Critical Essays on Langston Hughes* (Boston: G.K. Hall, 1986), pp. 191–9.

Bensussen Melia (ed.), *Blood Wedding and Yerma* (New York: TCG, 1994).

Bernheimer, Charles, and Claire Kahane (eds.), *In Dora's Case: Feminism, Hysteria, Feminism* (London: Virago, 1985).

Berry, Faith, *Langston Hughes: Before and Beyond Harlem* (Westport, Conn.: Lawrence Hill, 1983).

Binding, Paul, *Lorca: The Gay Imagination* (London: GMP, 1985).

Blum, Daniel, *A Pictorial History of the American Theatre 1860–1976*, enlarged and revised by John Willis (New York: Crown, 1977).

Buqueras y Bach, Ignacio, "Cataluña en Madrid: Marsillach-Pasqual," *ABC* (12 June 1988).

Burton, Julianne, "The Greatest Punishment: Female and Male in Lorca's Tragedies," in Beth Miller (ed.), *Women in Hispanic Literature* (Berkeley: University of California Press), pp. 259–79.

Colmeiro, José, Christina Dupláa, Patricia Greene, and Juana Sabadell (eds.), *Spain Today: Essays on Literature, Culture, Society* (Hanover, N.H.: Dartmouth College, 1995).

Crowley, Alice Lewisohn, *The Neighborhood Playhouse* (New York: Theater Arts, 1959).

de la Hera, Alberto, "Un afortunado cumpleaños," in *Guía del Ocio: especial CNTC* (no date [1996]), p. 3.

Dewell, Michael, and Carmen Zapata (trans.), *Federico García Lorca: Three Plays* (Harmondsworth: Penguin, 1992).

D'Lugo, Marvin, *The Films of Carlos Saura* (Princeton, N.J.: Princeton University Press, 1991).

Durán, Manuel, and Francesca Colecchia (eds.), *Lorca's Legacy: Essays on Lorca's Life, Poetry, and Theatre* (New York: Peter Lang, 1991).

Edwards, Gwynne (trans.), *García Lorca: Plays 2* (London: Methuen, 1990).

Efe, "Un desnudo teatral trae la polémica a la tranquila Turín," *ABC* (12 December 1986).

Enguídanos, Miguel, "Del rey de los gitanos al rey de Harlem: sobre *Poeta en Nueva York*," *Insula*, 476–7 (July–August 1986), 145–68.

Feal, Carlos, "El sacrificio de la hombría en *Bodas de sangre*," *MLN*, 99 (1984), 270–87.

Fernández Cifuentes, Luis, "*Yerma:* anatomía de una transgresión," *MLN*, 99 (1984), 288–307.

García Lorca en el teatro: la norma y la diferencia (Zaragoza: Universidad de Zaragoza, 1986).

"La verdad de la vida: Gibson versus Lorca," *Boletín de la Fundación Federico García Lorca*, 4 (1988), 102–13.

"Lorca en Nueva York: arquitecturas para un poeta," *Boletín de la Fundación de Federico García Lorca*, 10–11 (1992), 125–35.

Fernández Lera, Antonio (ed.), *Nuevas tendencias escénicas: la escritura teatral a debate* (Madrid: Ministerio de Cultura, 1985).

Foucault, Michel, *The History of Sexuality: An Introduction* (New York: Vintage, 1978).

Fraga Iribarne, Manuel, "Mil primaveras más para Cunqueiro," *Boletín de la Fundación Federico García Lorca*, 15 (1994), 13–14.

Frenk, Sue, Chris Perriam, and Mike Thompson, "The Literary Avantgarde: A Contradictory Modernity," in Helen Graham and Jo Labanyi, *Spanish Cultural Studies: An Introduction*, pp. 63–70 (p. 65).

Freud, Sigmund, *Case Histories I: "Dora" and "Little Hans,"* Penguin Freud Library, Vol. 8 (London: Penguin, 1990).

Case Histories II, Penguin Freud Library 9 (London: Penguin, 1991):
  "The Psychogenesis of a Case of Homosexuality in a Woman" (1920), pp. 367–400.

On Psychopathology, Penguin Freud Library 10 (London: Penguin, 1993):
  "On the Grounds for Detaching a Particular Syndrome from Neurasthenia under the Description 'Anxiety Neurosis'" (1895 [1894]), pp. 31–66.
  "My Views on the Part Played by Sexuality in the Etiology of the Neuroses" (1906 [1905]), pp. 67–82.
  "Hysterical Fantasies and Their Relation to Bisexuality" (1908), pp. 83–94.
  "Some General Remarks on Hysterical Attacks" (1909 [1908]), pp. 95–102.
  "Types of Onset of Neurosis" (1912), pp. 115–27.
  "The Disposition to Obsessional Neurosis" (1913), pp. 129–44.

"A Child Is Being Beaten (A Contribution to the Study of the Origin of Sexual Perversions)" (1919), pp. 159–94.

On Metapsychology, Penguin Freud Library 11 (London: Penguin, 1984): "Mourning and Melancholia" (1917 [1915]), pp. 245–68.

"The Economic Problem of Masochism" (1924), pp. 409–26.

"Negation" (1925), pp. 435–42.

"A Disturbance of Memory on the Acropolis" (1936), pp. 443–56.

and Josef Breuer, *Studies on Hysteria,* Penguin Freud Library 3 (London: Penguin, 1991).

Gallego Morell, Antonio, *Sobre García Lorca* (Granada: University of Granada, 1993).

Gallop, Jane, "Keys to Dora," in Charles Bernheimer and Claire Kahane (eds.), *In Dora's Case: Feminism, Hysteria, Feminism* (London: Virago, 1985), pp. 200–20.

García, Alejandro V., "Lorca y Granada sellan la reconciliación con la apertura del Museo de la Huerta de San Vicente," *El País* (11 May 1995).

García Lorca, Francisco, *Federico y su mundo* (Madrid: Alianza, 1981).

Gibson, Ian, *The Assassination of Federico García Lorca* (London: Penguin, 1983).

Federico García Lorca (Barcelona: Grijalbo, 1987).

Federico García Lorca: A Life (London: Faber, 1989).

Gide, André, *Corydon: édition augmentée* (Paris: Gallimard, 1924).

Gil, Ildefonso-Manuel, *Yerma,* 2nd ed. (Madrid: Cátedra, 1976).

Gilmour, John, "The Cross of Pain and Death: Religion in the Rural Tragedies," in Robert Havard (ed.), *Lorca: Poet and Playwright* (Cardiff: University of Wales, 1992), pp. 133–55.

Gossy, Mary S., *Freudian Slips: Woman, Writing, the Foreign Tongue* (Ann Arbor: University of Michigan Press, 1995).

Graham, Helen, and Jo Labanyi (eds.), *Spanish Cultural Studies: An Introduction: The Struggle for Modernity* (Oxford: Oxford University Press, 1995).

Granjel, Luis S., *Medicina española contemporánea* (Salamanca: Universidad de Salamanca, 1986).

Greenfield, Sumner M., "Lorca's Tragedies: Practice without Theory," *Siglo XX/20th Century,* 4.1–2 (1986–7), 1–5.

"El poeta de vuelta en España: lo neoyorquino en el teatro de Lorca, 1933–36," *Boletín de la Fundación de Federico García Lorca,* 10–11 (1992), 85–93.

Harris, Andrew B., *Broadway Theatre* (London and New York: Routledge, 1994).

Hartnoll, Phyllis (ed.), *Oxford Companion to the Theatre,* 4th ed. (Oxford: Oxford University Press, 1995).

Havard, Robert (ed.), *Lorca: Poet and Playwright* (Cardiff: University of Wales, 1992).

Hay, Samuel A., *African American Theatre* (Cambridge: Cambridge University Press, 1994).

Henderson, Mary C., *The City and the Theatre: New York Playhouses from Bowling Green to Times Square* (Clifton, N.J.: James T. White, 1973).

Hernández, Mario (ed.), *Bodas de sangre* (Madrid: Alianza, 1984).

Herrero, Javier, "The Father Against the Son: Lorca's Christian Vision," in Manuel Durán and Francesca Colecchia (eds.), *Lorca's Legacy* (New York: Peter Lang, 1991), pp. 1–20.

Higginbotham, Virginia, "*Así que pasen cinco años:* A Literary Version of *Un Chien andalou,*" in Manuel Durán and Francesca Colecchia (eds.), *Lorca's Legacy: Essays on Lorca's Life, Poetry, and Theater* (New York: Peter Lang, 1991), pp. 195–204.

Himelstein, Morgan Y., *Drama Was a Weapon: The Left-Wing Theater in New York 1929–41* (New Brunswick, N.J.: Rutgers University Press, 1963).

Hooper, John, *The New Spaniards,* revised edition (London: Penguin, 1995).

Hopewell, John, *El cine español después de Franco* (Madrid: El Arquero, 1989).

Huélamo Kosma, Julio, "La influencia de Freud en el teatro de García Lorca," *Boletín de la Fundación Federico García Lorca,* 6 (1989), 59–83.

Hughes, Langston, "Fate at the Wedding" [unpublished second draft of translation of *Bodas de sangre*] (New York Public Library, Billy Rose Collection: Call No. NCOF p.v. 359).

"Trouble with the Angels," *New Theatre* (July 1935), pp. 6–7.

"Mulatto" in Webster Smalley (ed.), *Five Plays* (Bloomington: Indiana University Press, 1963), pp. 1–42.

Selected Poems (London: Pluto, 1986).

Isaacs, Edith J.R., *The Negro in the American Theatre* (New York: Theatre Arts, 1947).

Jackson, Richard, "The Shared Vision of Langston Hughes and Black Hispanic Writers," *Black American Literature Forum,* 15.3 (1981), 89–92.

J.G.C., "El Ministerio de Cultura compra por 45 millones de pesetas el legado de Luis Buñuel," *ABC* (27 December 1995).

Jiménez Losantos, Federico, *Lo que queda de España* (Madrid: Temas de Hoy, 1995).

Johnston, David (ed. and trans.), *Yerma and the Love of Don Perlimplín for Belisa in the Garden* (London: Hodder and Stoughton, 1990).

"*Las terribles aduanas:* The Fortunes of Spanish Theatre in English," *Donaire,* 1 (September 1993), 18–24 (p. 21).

Josephs, Allen, and Juan Caballero (eds.), *Bodas de sangre* (Madrid: Cátedra, 1985).

Keller, Gary D., *The Significance and Impact of Gregorio Marañón* (New York: Bilingual Press, 1977).

Lacan, Jacques, "Fonction et champ de la parole et du langage en psychanalyse," in *Ecrits I* (Paris: Seuil, 1966), pp. 111–208.

"Le Stade du miroir comme formateur de la fonction du Je," in *Ecrits I* (Paris: Seuil, 1966), pp. 89–97.

Laffranque, Marie, *Les Idées esthétiques de Federico García Lorca* (Paris: Centre de Recherches Hispaniques, 1967).

Laín Entralgo, Pedro, *Gregorio Marañón: vida, obra, y persona* (Madrid: Espasa Calpe, 1979).

Laplanche, J., and J. B. Pontalis, *The Language of Psychoanalysis* (London: Karnak, 1988).

Lima, Robert, "Towards the Dionysiac: Pagan Elements and Rites in *Yerma,*" in Manuel Durán and Francesca Colecchia (eds.), *Lorca's Legacy: Essays on Lorca's Life, Poetry, and Theater* (New York: Peter Lang, 1991), pp. 115–34.

López, Silvia L., Jenaro Talens, and Darío Villanueva (eds.), *Critical Practices in Post-Franco Spain* (Minneapolis: University of Minnesota Press, 1994).

McMullen, Terence, "Federico Garía Lorca's Critique of Marriage in *Bodas de sangre,*" *Neophilologus,* 77 (1993), 61–73.

Marañón, Gregorio, *Biología y feminismo* (Madrid: Sucesor de Enrique Teodoro, 1920).

Patología e higiene de la emoción (Madrid: Sucesor de Enrique Teodoro, 1925).

Tres ensayos sobre la vida sexual, 3rd ed. (Madrid: Biblioteca Nueva, 1927).

Amor, conveniencia, y eugenesia (Madrid: Historia Nueva, 1929).

Los estados intersexuales en la especie humana (Madrid: Javier Morata, 1929).

El problema social de la infección (Madrid: El Libro del Pueblo, 1929).

Climaterio de la mujer y del hombre (Madrid: Espasa Calpe, 1937).

Amiel: un estudio sobre la timidez, 6th ed. (Madrid: Espasa Calpe, 1941).

"Diálogo antisocrático sobre *Corydon,*" in André Gide, *Corydon* (Madrid: Alianza, 1971), pp. 7–23.

Martínez Cerecedo, Adolfo, *Embarazo, parto, y puerperio* (Madrid: Ducazcal, 1904).

Martínez Lacalle, Guadalupe, "*Yerma:* 'Una tragedia pura y simplemente,'" *Neophilologus,* 72 (1988), 227–37.

Martínez Nadal, Rafael, *Lorca's "The Public": A Study of His Unfinished Play ("El Público") and of Love and Death in the Work of Federico García Lorca* (London: Calder and Boyars, 1974).

   Federico García Lorca: Autógrafos: II: El público, ed. Rafael Martínez Nadal (Oxford: Dolphin, 1976).

Matheus, John F., "Langston Hughes as Translator," in Therman B. O'Daniel (ed.), *Langston Hughes: Black Genius* (New York: William Morrow, 1971), pp. 157–70.

Maurer, Christopher, "Bach and *Bodas de sangre,*" in Manuel Durán and Francesca Colecchia (eds.), *Lorca's Legacy* (New York: Peter Lang, 1991), pp. 103–14.

Maurer, Christopher (ed.), *Federico García Lorca: Poet in New York* (London: Penguin, 1990).

   (ed.), *Federico García Lorca: Prosa inédita de juventud* (Madrid: Cátedra, 1994).

Millán, María Clementa (ed.), *El público* (Madrid: Cátedra, 1987).

Miralles, Alberto, "La progresiva domesticación de la vanguardia teatral durante la transición política española," in Antonio Fernández Lera (ed.), *Nuevas tendencias escénicas: la escritura teatral a debate* (Madrid: Ministerio de Cultura, 1985), pp. 26–30.

Molina Foix, Vicente, *El cine estilográfico: crítica recogida 1981–93* (Barcelona: Anagrama, 1993).

Monegal, Antonio, "Unmasking the Maskuline [*sic*]: Transvestism and Tragedy in García Lorca's *El público,*" *MLN,* 109 (1994), 204–16.

Monegal, Antonio (ed.), *Viaje a la luna* (Valencia: Pre-textos, 1994).

Mullen, Edward J. (ed.), *Critical Essays on Langston Hughes* (Boston: G.K. Hall, 1986).

   "Langston Hughes in Mexico and Cuba," *Review: Latin American Literature and Arts,* 47 (Fall 1993), 23–7.

Muñoz-Rojas, Ritama, "Lorca entra por primera vez en el teatro de La Latina," *El País* (17 September 1995).

O'Daniel, Therman B. (ed.), *Langston Hughes: Black Genius* (New York: William Morrow, 1971).

O'Neil, Nance, unpublished scrapbook (New York Public Library, Billy Rose Collection: Call No. MWEZ X n.c. 19877).

Ortega, José, "El gitano y el negro en la poesía de García Lorca," *Cuadernos Hispanoamericanos,* 433–4 (1986), 145–68.

Paepe, Christian de (ed.), *Federico García Lorca: Poesía inédita de juventud* (Madrid: Cátedra, 1994).

Parker, Fiona, and Terence McMullan, "Federico García Lorca's *Yerma* and the World of Work," *Neophilologus*, 74 (1990), 58–69.

Pascual, Itziar, "La escritura española de este siglo, apuesta del Centro Dramático Nacional," *El Mundo* (5 September 1995).

Pérez Coterillo, Moisés, "La escritura teatral: marco para un debate," in Antonio Fernández Lera (ed.), *Nuevas tendencias escénicas: la escritura teatral a debate* (Madrid: Ministerio de Cultura, 1985), pp. 14–20.

Perriam, Chris, *Desire and Dissent: An Introduction to Luis Antonio de Villena* (Oxford: Berg, 1995).

Pulido, Natividad, "El Estado adquiere los textos inéditos de Lorca por casi cinco millones de pesetas: Alborch decidirá si van a la Biblioteca Nacional o a la Fundación del poeta," *ABC* (21 February 1995).

Quiñonero, Juan Pedro, "Martirio y Ketama reinventan la tradición flamenca en París," *ABC* (6 April 1988).

Rampersad, Arnold, "Langston Hughes and His Critics on the Left," *Langston Hughes Review*, 5.2 (1986), 34–40.

The Life of Langston Hughes (Cambridge: Cambridge University Press, 1986–8).

Ramsden, H. (ed.), *Bodas de sangre* (Manchester, England: Manchester University Press, 1980).

Ricks, Sybil Ray, "A Textual Comparison of Langston Hughes's *Mulatto*, 'Father and Son,' and 'The Barrier,'" *Black American Literature Forum*, 15.3 (1981), 101–3.

Roses-Lozano, Joaquín, "Códigos sígnicos y discurso teatral en *Así que pasen cinco años*," *Anales de la Literatura Española Contemporánea*, 14 (1989), 115–41.

Ruiz Portella, Javier (ed.), *Federico García Lorca: Sonetos del amor oscuro; Poemas de amor y erotismo; Inéditos de madurez* (Barcelona: Altera, 1995).

Salas, Roger, "Joaquín Cortés deslumbra con 'Pasión gitana': el espectáculo lleva ell ballet flamenco hacia nuevos horizontes," *El País* (9 September 1995).

Sarabia y Pardo, Jesús, *Estudio higiénico-médico de las casas de maternidad* (Madrid: R. Velasco, 1893).

Savater, Fernando, *Etica como amor propio* (Barcelona: Grijalbo Mondadori, 1995).

Scanlon, Geraldine, *La polémica feminista en España contemporánea* (Madrid: Akal, 1986).

Schonberg, Jean-Louis, *Federico García Lorca: l'homme, l'oeuvre* (Paris: Plon, 1956).

A la recherche de Lorca (Neuchâtel: Baconnière, 1966).

Serrano Carrasco, Cristina, *La casa de Bernarda Alba*, Apuntes Cúpula (Barcelona: CEAC, 1989).

Sinfield, Alan, *The Wilde Century: Effeminacy, Oscar Wilde, and the Queer Moment* (London: Cassell, 1994).

Smith, Paul Julian, "Lorca and Foucault," in *The Body Hispanic: Gender and Sexuality in Spanish and Spanish American Literature* (Oxford: Oxford University Press, 1989), pp. 105–37.

Laws of Desire: Questions of Homosexuality in Spanish Writing and Film 1960–90 (Oxford: Oxford University Press, 1992).

García Lorca/Almodóvar: Gender, Nationality, and the Limits of the Visible (Cambridge: Cambridge University Press, 1995).

Vision Machines: Cinema, Literature, and Sexuality in Spain and Cuba, 1983–93 (London: Verso, 1996).

Soler y Soto, Luis, "La maternidad," in *Discursos leídos en la Sociedad Española de Higiene en la sesión inaugural del año académico de 1936* (Madrid: J. Cosano, 1936), pp. 21–33.

Soria Olmedo, Andrés (ed.), *Federico García Lorca: Teatro inédito de juventud* (Madrid: Cátedra, 1994).

Stainton, Leslie, "A Concept of Land: José Luis Gómez, Lorca, and *Bodas de sangre*," *Anales de la Literatura Española Contemporánea*, 11 (1986), 205–13.

Tambling, Jeremy, *Confession: Sexuality, Sin, the Subject* (Manchester, England: Manchester University Press, 1990).

Tapia, J.L., "La Fundación García Lorca rechaza su traslado a Granada," *Ideal* (5 April 1996).

Taylor, Diana, and Juan Villegas (eds.), *Negotiating Performance: Gender, Sexuality, and Theatricality in Latin/o America* (Durham, N.C.: Duke University Press, 1995).

Torres, Augusto M., *Diccionario del cine español* (Madrid: Espasa Calpe, 1994).

"The Film Industry: Under Pressure from the State and Television," in Helen Graham and Jo Labanyi (eds.), *Spanish Cultural Studies: An Introduction* (Oxford: Oxford University Press, 1995), pp. 369–73.

Ucelay, Margarita (ed.), *Así que pasen cinco años: leyenda del tiempo* (Madrid: Cátedra, 1995).

Vallés Copeiro del Villa, Antonio, *Historia de la política de fomento del cine español* (Valencia: Universidad de Valencia, 1992).

Ventura Pastor, Joseph, *Discurso médico chirúrgico sobre los depósitos lácteos o leche extraviada en las mugeres embarazadas* (Madrid: Viuda de Ibarra, 1793).

Vidal Solares, Francisco, *Preceptos acerca del embarazo, parto, y puerperio* (Barcelona: J. Horta, 1909).

Vilches de Frutos, María Francisca, and Dru Dougherty (eds.), *Los estrenos teatrales de Federico García Lorca* (Madrid: Tabapress, 1992).

Villanueva, Darío, "The Evolution of the Spanish Literary System," in José Colmeiro, Christina Dupláa, Patricia Greene, and Juana Sabadell (eds.), *Spain Today: Essays on Literature, Culture, Society* (Hanover, N.H.: Dartmouth College Press, 1995), pp. 139–47.

Villena, Luis Antonio de, "La sensibilidad homoerótica en el *Romancero gitano*," *Campus*, 11 (December 1986), 27–30.

Warner, Robin (ed.), *Yerma* (Manchester, England: Manchester University Press, 1994).

Weber, Jean-Paul, *Genèse de l'âme poétique* (Paris: Gallimard, 1961).

Domaines thématiques (Paris: Gallimard, 1963).

Weissberger, José, "Bitter Oleander" [unpublished translation of *Bodas de sangre*] (New York Public Library, Billy Rose Collection: Call No. NCOF p.v. 359).

West, Cornell, *Race Matters* (Boston: Beacon, 1992).

Keeping Faith: Philosophy and Race in America (New York and London: Routledge, 1993).

Ytak, (*sic*), *Lluís Pasqual: Camí de teatre* (Barcelona: Alter Pirene Escene, 1994).

Zatlin, Phyllis, *Cross-Cultural Approaches to Theatre: The Spanish–French Connection* (Metuchen, N.J., and London: Scarecrow Press, 1994).

Zdenek, Josef W., "Alter Ego and Personality Projection in García Lorca's *Así que pasen cinco años*," *Revista de Estudios Hispánicos*, 16 (1982), 303–13.

Index

Note: References to figures are followed by "f."

183

Lightning Source UK Ltd.
Milton Keynes UK
UKOW04f0926270815

257628UK00001B/35/P